Rome Travel Guide

Discover the Eternal City: Insider Tips, Hidden Gems, and Must-See Highlights for Every Traveler. Pocket Edition

Ginevra Costa

© Copyright 2025 by Ginevra Costa
All rights reserved

This document is geared towards providing exact and reliable information with regards to the topic and issue covered. The publication is sold with the idea that the publisher is not required to render accounting, officially permitted, or otherwise, qualified services. If advice is necessary, legal or professional, a practiced individual in the profession should be ordered.

From a Declaration of Principles which was accepted and approved equally by a Committee of the American Bar Association and a Committee of Publishers and Associations.

In no way is it legal to reproduce, duplicate, or transmit any part of this document in either electronic means or in printed format. Recording of this publication is strictly prohibited and any storage of this document is not allowed unless with written permission from the publisher. All rights reserved.

The information provided herein is stated to be truthful and consistent, in that any liability, in terms of inattention or otherwise, by any usage or abuse of any policies, processes, or directions contained within is the solitary and utter responsibility of the recipient reader. Under no circumstances will any legal responsibility or blame be held against the publisher for any reparation, damages, or monetary loss due to the information herein, either directly or indirectly.

Respective authors own all copyrights not held by the publisher.

The information herein is offered for informational purposes solely, and is universal as so. The presentation of the information is without contract or any type of guarantee assurance.

The trademarks that are used are without any consent, and the publication of the trademark is without permission or backing by the trademark owner. All trademarks and brands within this book are for clarifying purposes only and are the owned by the owners themselves, not affiliated with this document.

TABLE OF CONTENTS

Introduction 7
    Why Visit Rome?.. 7
    How to Use This Guide 10
    A Brief History of the Eternal City.......................................14
    The Best Time to Visit Rome 18
    Essentials to Pack for Your Roman Adventure 21

Chapter 1: Planning Your Trip to Rome............................... 26
    Choosing the Right Area to Stay: Rome's Best Neighborhoods 26
    The Ultimate Packing Checklist for Rome 30
    Budgeting for Your Trip: From Luxury to Budget-Friendly Travel 34
    Navigating Rome's Transportation: Airports, Trains, and Public Transit 38
    Safety and Travel Tips: Staying Safe in a Busy City.............42

Chapter 2: Must-See Landmarks in Rome 46
    The Colosseum: A Step Back in Time 46
    The Roman Forum and Palatine Hill 50
    St. Peter's Basilica: A Spiritual Masterpiece.........................53
    The Vatican Museums and the Sistine Chapel 57
    The Pantheon: Ancient Architecture at Its Finest................62
    Trevi Fountain: Tossing Coins and Its Legends 65
    Piazza Navona: Rome's Open-Air Gallery............................69
    Castel Sant'Angelo: Fortress, Museum, and History Combined.........73

Chapter 3: Hidden Gems and Off-the-Beaten-Path Adventures ... 78
    The Aventine Keyhole: A Secret View of St. Peter's Dome ..78
    Trastevere: Rome's Bohemian Neighborhood 81

Testaccio Market: A Foodie's Paradise.. 85

San Clemente Basilica: A Journey Through Layers of History........... 89

The Catacombs of Rome: Exploring Underground Mysteries........... 93

The Appian Way: Ancient Roads and Aqueducts................................ 97

Villa Doria Pamphili: Rome's Largest Public Park 100

Chapter 4: Exploring Rome's Art and Architecture 105

Baroque Marvels: Bernini and Borromini's Masterpieces 105

Renaissance Rome: Michelangelo's Influence................................ 109

Caravaggio's Masterpieces in Roman Churches 113

Contemporary Art in the Eternal City... 116

The Beauty of Roman Fountains 121

Rome's Obelisks: Ancient Egypt in Italy 125

Chapter 5: Rome's Culinary Scene.. 130

Traditional Roman Dishes You Must Try 130

The Best Pizzerias and Gelaterias in Rome..................................... 134

Wine and Aperitivo Culture: How to Drink Like a Roman 138

Food Markets to Explore: Campo de' Fiori, Testaccio, and More.... 141

Vegetarian and Vegan Options in a Meat-Heavy City..................... 145

Dining Etiquette in Rome: Tips for Eating Out................................. 150

Chapter 6: Rome by Night 154

Evening Strolls: The Magic of Rome's Illuminated Landmarks........ 154

Nightlife Hotspots: Bars, Clubs, and Live Music.............................. 158

Evening Dining: Late-Night Eats and Romantic Restaurants 162

Night Tours of Rome: A Unique Perspective After Dark 165

Special Events and Festivals: Rome's Nightlife Calendar 170

Chapter 7: Final Tips and Resources.. 175

How to Avoid Travel Burnout in Rome 175
Souvenirs Worth Bringing Home 179
Emergency Contacts and Local Support 183
Recommended Books and Movies About Rome 187
Farewell to the Eternal City: Leaving with Lasting Memories 191

Conclusion... 195

Embracing the Eternal City: A Reflection 195
Staying Connected with Rome: Future Adventures......................... 198

BONUS 1: Essential phrases for your daily travel needs in Rome 202

BONUS 2: Printable travel journal 203

BONUS 3: 10 tips "that can save the day" on your trip in Rome 204

INTRODUCTION

Why Visit Rome?

Rome, the Eternal City, is a destination that beckons travelers with its unparalleled blend of history, art, culture, and vibrant modern life. There is no other city in the world where ancient ruins stand shoulder to shoulder with Renaissance palaces and bustling piazzas, creating a living museum that invites you to lose yourself in its cobblestone streets. Every corner reveals a story, every building whispers secrets of centuries past, and every meal is a celebration of Italian culinary mastery. From the grandeur of its landmarks to the intimacy of its hidden alleys, Rome captures the imagination and leaves an indelible mark on the heart of every visitor.

The city's history stretches back over 2,500 years, making it one of the most historically significant places on the planet. Rome was the epicenter of the mighty Roman Empire, whose influence shaped laws, governance, and architecture across continents. Walking through the city is akin to stepping into a time machine; the Colosseum echoes with the roars of ancient gladiatorial battles, and the Roman Forum still carries the weight of political debates that determined the fate of empires. The Pantheon, with its awe-inspiring dome, stands as a testament to Roman engineering prowess, while the Appian Way, one of the oldest roads in the world, offers a tangible connection to the past. This layering of history is not confined to the ancient world; the Renaissance and Baroque periods left an equally indelible imprint, with artists like Michelangelo, Bernini, and Caravaggio bringing their genius to bear on the city's fabric. Rome is a city where history is not just preserved but lived—it is in the air you breathe and the stones beneath your feet.

Art and architecture enthusiasts will find Rome to be an unparalleled treasure trove. The Vatican Museums house one of the most extensive and impressive collections of art in the world, culminating in the Sistine Chapel, where Michelangelo's ceiling frescoes leave visitors speechless. St. Peter's Basilica, with its ornate interiors and towering dome, showcases the pinnacle of Renaissance architecture and offers breathtaking views of the city from its rooftop. But Rome's artistic offerings are not confined to museums and churches; they spill out into the streets. Piazza Navona is adorned with Bernini's Fountain of the Four Rivers, a masterpiece of Baroque sculpture, while the Trevi Fountain, with its dramatic cascades of water and intricate carvings, is a magnet for those wishing to toss a coin and ensure their return to the city. Even the city's everyday structures, like its bridges and aqueducts, are imbued with a beauty and functionality that speak to centuries of architectural innovation.

Rome is not merely a relic of the past; it is a vibrant, living city that pulses with energy and modernity. Its neighborhoods each have their own distinct character, from the bohemian charm of Trastevere to the upscale elegance of the Spanish Steps area. Romans are known for their zest for life, and this is evident in their daily routines, whether it's sipping an espresso at a bustling café, enjoying a leisurely aperitivo in a sunlit piazza, or cheering on their favorite football team at the Stadio Olimpico. The city's markets, such as Campo de' Fiori and Testaccio, provide a sensory overload with their colorful displays of fresh produce, aromatic spices, and local delicacies. Exploring these markets offers a glimpse into the everyday lives of Romans and an opportunity to taste the ingredients that make Italian cuisine so renowned.

Food is undeniably one of Rome's greatest attractions. The city's culinary scene is a celebration of simplicity and quality, with traditional dishes that have stood the test of time. Cacio e pepe, a creamy pasta dish made with pecorino cheese and black pepper, exemplifies the Roman philosophy of letting a few high-quality ingredients shine. Carbonara, amatriciana, and carciofi alla romana (Roman-style artichokes) are just a few of the other iconic dishes that await food lovers. Street food options, such as supplì (fried rice balls) and pizza al taglio (pizza by the slice), offer quick and delicious ways to refuel during a day of sightseeing. For those with a sweet tooth, gelato shops abound, each vying to offer the creamiest, most flavorful scoops. Dining in Rome is not just about the food; it's about the experience. Meals are savored slowly, accompanied by laughter, conversation, and perhaps a glass of local wine.

Rome's appeal extends to its climate, which is one of the most pleasant in Europe. The city enjoys a Mediterranean climate, with mild winters and hot, sunny summers. Spring and autumn are particularly delightful times to visit, as the weather is warm but not oppressive, and the city's gardens and parks burst into bloom. Villa Borghese, a sprawling park in the heart of Rome, offers a green oasis where visitors can escape the hustle and bustle of the city, rent a bike, or simply relax under the shade of a tree. The Tiber River, which snakes through the city, is another scenic spot for leisurely strolls, especially during the golden hour when the setting sun casts a warm glow over the water and the surrounding buildings.

For those seeking spiritual or religious experiences, Rome holds a special significance. As the center of the Roman Catholic Church, the city attracts pilgrims from around the world. St. Peter's Square, with its massive colonnades and the Pope's residence, is a place of profound reverence and awe. The city is also home to numerous ancient churches, each with its own unique history and artistic treasures. From the mosaics of Santa Maria in Trastevere to the frescoes of San Luigi dei Francesi, these sacred spaces offer moments of tranquility and reflection amidst the city's hustle and bustle.

Rome's allure is also in its ability to surprise and delight. Beyond the famous landmarks and well-trodden tourist paths lie countless hidden gems waiting to be discovered. A quiet courtyard, a hidden garden, or an unassuming trattoria serving the best meal of your life—these are the moments that make a trip to Rome truly unforgettable. The city's layers of history and culture mean that there is always something new to uncover, no matter how many times you visit.

What truly sets Rome apart is its ability to make every visitor feel a part of its story. The city's blend of ancient and modern, its celebration of art and life, and its warm and welcoming people create an atmosphere that is both inspiring and comforting. Rome is a city that invites you to slow down, to savor the moment, and to appreciate the beauty in the everyday. Whether it's your first visit or your fifteenth, the Eternal City has a way of capturing your heart and calling you back for more.

How to Use This Guide

This guide has been carefully designed to be your ultimate companion in discovering everything Rome has to offer, regardless of your travel style, interests, or experience level. Whether this is your first time in the Eternal City or you're returning to uncover new layers of its charm, the structure and content of this book will help you navigate, plan, and savor your Roman adventure with ease. Each section has been crafted to provide practical, actionable information, insider tips, and cultural insights, ensuring you can make the most of your time in one of the world's most captivating cities.

The first step to using this guide effectively is understanding its layout. Each chapter is dedicated to a specific aspect of your journey, progressing logically from pre-trip planning to your final moments in Rome. This ensures you have all the information you need at each stage of your adventure. By starting with advice on planning your trip, such as choosing where to stay, what to pack, and how to budget, you can set a solid foundation before you even arrive. Once in Rome, the chapters take you through must-see landmarks, hidden gems, art and architecture, culinary delights, and the vibrant nightlife of the city. Finally, the guide concludes with essential tips for winding down your visit and leaving with meaningful memories.

To get the most out of this guide, it's helpful to read some sections before your trip and revisit others once you're in the city. For example, the chapter on planning your trip will be most useful during the early stages of organizing your holiday. This includes information on where to stay, from the bustling streets of the historic center to the quieter, more residential neighborhoods like Monteverde or Aventine. Each area offers unique experiences, and this guide breaks down their characteristics to help you choose the one that suits your needs. Similarly, the packing list and budgeting tips will help ensure you're fully prepared without overpacking or overspending, leaving you free to enjoy the journey with peace of mind.

Once you've landed in Rome, this guide becomes your on-the-ground resource for exploring the city. The chapters covering must-see landmarks and hidden gems provide detailed descriptions of each site, along with historical context, insider tips, and practical advice for navigating crowds and accessing lesser-known features. For example, while visiting the Colosseum, you'll not only learn about its storied history but also discover the best times to visit, how to skip the lines, and nearby spots that complement your experience. The same goes for hidden gems like the Aventine Keyhole, where you'll find tips on how to reach it, how to time your visit for the best view, and what makes this secret spot so special.

This guide is more than just a collection of facts and recommendations; it's also a tool for immersing yourself in Roman culture and traditions. The sections on food, art, and local customs are designed to enhance your understanding of the city, transforming your experience from that of a casual tourist to a more engaged traveler. For instance, you'll find advice on how to order coffee like a local, what to expect when dining out, and how to participate in the beloved Roman ritual of aperitivo. Understanding these cultural nuances will not only enrich your trip but also make interactions with locals more enjoyable and authentic.

Flexibility is key when using this guide. While it's a comprehensive resource, it's not meant to dictate a rigid itinerary. Rome is a city that rewards spontaneity, and some of your most memorable experiences may come from simply wandering its streets and stumbling upon unexpected treasures. That said, the guide is here to provide structure and inspiration when needed. If you're overwhelmed by the sheer number of things to see and do, the chapters on landmarks and hidden gems can help you prioritize. On the other hand, if you have a specific interest, such as Renaissance art or Roman cuisine, you can dive into the relevant sections for a more focused exploration.

This guide also includes practical information to help you navigate the city with confidence. The chapter on transportation provides clear explanations of how to use Rome's buses, trams, and metro system, as well as tips for walking in a city where ancient ruins and winding alleys often defy modern maps. You'll also find advice on staying safe, from avoiding pickpockets in crowded areas to understanding local traffic patterns as a pedestrian. These practical details are essential for ensuring your trip runs smoothly, allowing you to focus on enjoying the sights and sounds of Rome.

One of the unique features of this guide is its emphasis on both iconic attractions and lesser-known experiences. While it's important to visit landmarks like the Vatican and the Trevi Fountain, this guide also encourages you to venture off the beaten path. By exploring neighborhoods like Trastevere or Testaccio, you'll gain a deeper appreciation of Rome's diverse character and discover a side of the city that many tourists miss. The recommendations for hidden gems are based on local knowledge and personal experiences, offering you a chance to see Rome through the eyes of those who live there.

The bonus sections at the end of this guide are designed to add even more value to your trip. From essential Italian phrases to printable travel journal templates, these extras provide tools to enhance your experience and help you stay organized. The tips for handling unexpected situations, like dealing with lost luggage or navigating a language barrier, are particularly useful for first-time travelers. By preparing for these scenarios in advance, you'll be better equipped to handle them with confidence and ease.

It's also worth noting that this guide is adaptable to different travel styles and preferences. Whether you're a solo traveler, a couple on a romantic getaway, or a family with young children, you'll find tips and recommendations tailored to your needs. For example, families might appreciate the suggestions for kid-friendly activities and restaurants, while solo travelers can benefit from safety tips and ideas for meeting fellow adventurers. This inclusivity ensures that the guide is relevant and useful for a wide range of readers.

To fully enjoy all that this guide has to offer, take your time exploring its pages and let it inspire your journey. Use it as a roadmap, a reference, and a source of inspiration, but don't be afraid to deviate from its suggestions if something else catches your eye. Rome is a city that thrives on serendipity, and some of your best memories may come from following your instincts rather than a plan. At the same time, this guide is here to ensure that you're informed, prepared, and empowered to make the most of your time in the Eternal City.

This guide is not just about providing information; it's about enhancing your connection to Rome. It invites you to engage with the city on a deeper level, to appreciate its history and culture, and to create your own unique memories. Whether you're marveling at the grandeur of the Colosseum, savoring a perfectly cooked plate of pasta, or simply sitting in a quiet piazza watching the world go by, this guide is here to support and inspire you every step of the way.

A Brief History of the Eternal City

Rome's history is a tapestry woven with threads of power, artistry, faith, and innovation, stretching back over 2,700 years. Founded, according to legend, in 753 BCE by Romulus and Remus, twin brothers raised by a she-wolf, Rome began as a small settlement on the Palatine Hill. This mythic origin story, while shrouded in mystery and symbolism, reflects the city's enduring identity as a place of resilience and ambition. What started as a humble cluster of huts eventually grew into the epicenter of one of the most influential civilizations the world has ever known.

The early days of Rome were marked by its establishment as a monarchy. From its founding, Rome was ruled by a series of kings, both of Latin and Etruscan origin, who played a formative role in shaping the city. The Etruscans, particularly, left a lasting imprint on Roman culture, introducing architectural techniques like the arch and influencing religious practices. During this era, the Forum Romanum, or Roman Forum, began to take shape as the heart of civic and religious life. However, dissatisfaction with the monarchy's rule led to a seismic shift in governance. In 509 BCE, Rome transitioned to a republic, a monumental step that laid the groundwork for its future as a dominant power.

The Roman Republic was a period of remarkable political innovation. Governed by elected officials and a complex system of checks and balances, it was during this time that Rome began its expansion beyond its immediate surroundings. The Republic's military campaigns were relentless and highly strategic, eventually bringing the Italian Peninsula under Roman control. The legions, disciplined and efficient, became the backbone of Rome's dominance. The republic wasn't without its flaws; internal conflicts, particularly between the patricians (the aristocratic elite) and the plebeians (the common people), often threatened its stability. However, these struggles also led to legal reforms, such as the Twelve Tables, which served as Rome's first code of law and a precursor to modern legal systems.

The Republic's expansionism brought it into contact—and conflict—with other powerful civilizations. The Punic Wars against Carthage were a defining series of battles that demonstrated Rome's military might. The most famous of these conflicts was the Second Punic War, during which the Carthaginian general Hannibal crossed the Alps with elephants to invade Italy. Despite his early victories, Rome ultimately triumphed, securing its dominance over the western Mediterranean. This victory marked the beginning of Rome's transformation into a global superpower, as territories from Spain to Greece and North Africa became part of its growing empire.

The successes of the Republic, however, sowed the seeds of internal discord. The vast wealth and territories acquired through conquest exacerbated inequalities within Roman society. Political corruption and power struggles became rampant, leading to a series of civil wars. Figures like Julius Caesar, Pompey, and Crassus rose to prominence during this turbulent period. Caesar, in particular, played a pivotal role in the Republic's downfall. His crossing of the Rubicon River in 49 BCE was an act of defiance that led to a civil war and ultimately his appointment as dictator for life. While his assassination in 44 BCE was intended to restore the Republic, it instead plunged Rome into further chaos.

Out of this chaos emerged the Roman Empire, heralded by the rise of Augustus (formerly Octavian), Caesar's adopted heir. In 27 BCE, Augustus declared himself the first emperor, marking the beginning of an era known as the Pax Romana, or Roman Peace. This period, lasting over two centuries, was characterized by stability, economic prosperity, and cultural flourishing. Rome reached the height of its power, with its territories stretching from Britain to the Middle East. Monumental architecture such as the Colosseum, the Pantheon, and aqueducts symbolized the empire's grandeur and engineering prowess. The city itself became a hub of commerce, art, and innovation, with a population that swelled to over a million people.

Religion played a significant role in the empire's cohesion. Initially, Roman religion was polytheistic, heavily influenced by Greek mythology. Temples dedicated to gods like Jupiter, Venus, and Mars dotted the cityscape. Over time, however, new religious movements began to take root. Christianity, initially a persecuted sect, gained followers throughout the empire. The pivotal moment came in 313 CE, when Emperor Constantine issued the Edict of Milan, granting religious tolerance and effectively ending the persecution of Christians. Constantine's subsequent establishment of Constantinople as a second capital marked a shift in the empire's focus, but Rome remained a spiritual and cultural center.

The decline of the Roman Empire is a story of both external pressures and internal decay. By the 4th and 5th centuries CE, the empire faced invasions from Germanic tribes, economic instability, and administrative challenges. In 476 CE, the Western Roman Empire officially fell, an event often seen as the end of antiquity and the beginning of the Middle Ages. However, Rome's legacy was far from extinguished. The Eastern Roman Empire, or Byzantine Empire, continued for nearly a thousand years, and the city of Rome itself became the seat of the papacy, ensuring its continued influence.

During the Middle Ages, Rome underwent significant transformation. The grandeur of the ancient city gave way to a more modest existence, as many of its monumental structures fell into disrepair. Yet, it remained an important religious center, with the Catholic Church playing a central role in European politics and culture. The construction of St. Peter's Basilica and other churches signified Rome's enduring spiritual importance. By the time of the Renaissance, Rome experienced a rebirth of its own, fueled by the patronage of powerful popes like Julius II and Leo X.

The Renaissance brought a renewed focus on art, architecture, and humanism. Michelangelo, Raphael, and Bramante were among the luminaries who contributed to Rome's transformation during this period. The Sistine Chapel, Vatican Museums, and numerous palaces and fountains are lasting testaments to this era of creativity. Rome became a magnet for artists and intellectuals, solidifying its reputation as a cultural capital.

The Baroque period further embellished the city. Gian Lorenzo Bernini and Francesco Borromini left their mark with dramatic sculptures, churches, and fountains that continue to define Rome's aesthetic. The city's streetscapes were reimagined with grand piazzas and sweeping vistas, creating a theatrical experience that continues to captivate visitors.

Modern Rome emerged in the 19th and 20th centuries, as Italy unified and Rome was declared its capital in 1871. The city underwent significant urban development, balancing its ancient heritage with the needs of a growing modern population. The fascist era under Mussolini saw the construction of new districts like EUR, designed to reflect the regime's ideology. Post-World War II, Rome embraced democracy and became a symbol of Italian identity and resilience.

Today, Rome is a city where the past and present coexist in remarkable harmony. Ancient ruins stand alongside Renaissance masterpieces and bustling modern streets. Its history is not confined to textbooks or museum exhibits; it is alive in every piazza, every cobblestone, and every conversation. Rome's story is one of continuity and reinvention, a testament to the enduring power of a city that has shaped—and been shaped by—the world.

The Best Time to Visit Rome

Rome is a city that can captivate visitors at any time of the year, but choosing the right time to visit can significantly impact your experience. The Eternal City, with its centuries-old ruins, bustling piazzas, and rich cultural tapestry, offers something unique in every season. Understanding the nuances of Rome's climate, crowd patterns, and seasonal events will help you tailor your trip to your preferences and ensure you make the most of your time exploring its wonders.

Spring is one of the most popular seasons to visit Rome, and with good reason. From March to May, the city awakens from the quieter winter months with a renewed energy. The weather during this time is pleasantly mild, with daytime temperatures ranging between 15°C and 20°C (59°F to 68°F). These conditions are ideal for long days of sightseeing, as you can comfortably wander through the ruins of the Roman Forum, climb the steps to Piazza del Campidoglio, or stroll along the Tiber River without the oppressive heat of summer. The city's greenery comes to life during this period, with parks like Villa Borghese and Villa Doria Pamphili bursting into bloom. Wisteria vines drape over archways, and the sight of cherry blossoms around the Palatine Hill adds a romantic touch to the landscape.

Spring also brings a variety of cultural and religious events that add depth to your visit. Easter, which often falls in April, is a particularly significant time in Rome, as it is the heart of Catholicism. St. Peter's Basilica becomes the focal point of Holy Week celebrations, culminating in the Pope's Easter Sunday Mass. While these events are deeply moving, they also draw large crowds, so it's important to plan accordingly. If you wish to attend, arrive early and be prepared for heightened security and bustling public spaces. Beyond Easter, the city hosts numerous spring festivals, such as the Natale di Roma on April 21st, which marks the founding of Rome. This celebration includes historical reenactments, parades, and fireworks, offering a glimpse into the city's ancient traditions.

Summer in Rome, spanning from June to August, is both vibrant and challenging. The long, sunny days provide ample opportunity to explore the city's outdoor attractions, but the heat can be intense, often exceeding 30°C (86°F) in July and August. If you plan to visit during the summer, it's essential to adapt your itinerary to the climate. Start your day early to take advantage of cooler mornings, and prioritize indoor activities like visiting the Vatican Museums or the Capitoline Museums during the peak afternoon heat. Many Romans themselves escape the city in August for their annual vacations, leading to a quieter atmosphere in some areas but also the closure of certain local businesses and restaurants.

Despite the heat, summer is a season of lively cultural events and outdoor experiences. The Estate Romana, or Roman Summer, transforms the city into an open-air festival, with concerts, theater performances, and film screenings held in iconic locations like Castel Sant'Angelo and Piazza Vittorio. The Isola del Cinema, an open-air film festival on Tiber Island, is a favorite among locals and visitors alike. For those seeking a unique perspective of Rome, consider an evening visit to landmarks like the Colosseum or the Vatican Museums, both of which offer special nighttime tours during the summer months. The illuminated cityscape takes on a magical quality after dark, making it one of the most enchanting times to explore.

Autumn, from September to November, rivals spring as one of the best times to visit Rome. The oppressive heat of summer fades, giving way to cooler temperatures that hover around 20°C (68°F) in September and gradually decline to 14°C (57°F) in November. The city regains its rhythm as locals return from their vacations, and a sense of authenticity permeates the streets. Autumn also marks the harvest season in Italy, making it an excellent time to indulge in Roman cuisine. Truffles, chestnuts, and porcini mushrooms feature prominently on seasonal menus, and wine festivals in and around the city celebrate the grape harvest.

Cultural life in Rome thrives in the autumn months. The Rome Film Festival, held in October, attracts international attention with its screenings and celebrity appearances. Art lovers will appreciate the numerous exhibitions hosted by the city's galleries and museums, many of which unveil new collections during this period. The cooler weather is perfect for outdoor exploration, whether you're wandering through the narrow streets of Trastevere or taking a day trip to the ancient ruins of Ostia Antica. The golden hues of autumn foliage provide a picturesque backdrop for your adventures, adding a touch of warmth to the city's timeless beauty.

Winter in Rome, from December to February, offers a quieter and more intimate experience. While temperatures can dip to around 8°C (46°F) during the day and occasionally lower at night, the city rarely sees snowfall, and the crisp air is invigorating rather than harsh. Winter is the low season for tourism, which means fewer crowds at major attractions and more opportunities to explore at your own pace. Imagine standing before the grandeur of the Pantheon without jostling for space or taking your time to admire the intricate details of the Trevi Fountain without feeling rushed. The quieter streets also allow for more meaningful interactions with locals, whether you're chatting with a vendor at Campo de' Fiori or sharing a meal in a family-run trattoria.

The holiday season brings its own charm to Rome. Christmas markets pop up in piazzas, with Piazza Navona hosting one of the most famous. The city's churches display elaborate nativity scenes, and St. Peter's Square features a towering Christmas tree and a life-sized nativity scene that draw visitors from around the world. Midnight Mass at St. Peter's Basilica on Christmas Eve is a profound experience, though it requires advance planning to secure tickets. As the year comes to a close, Rome celebrates New Year's Eve with fireworks, concerts, and festivities that light up the city. January and February, while quieter, are excellent months for museum visits and enjoying hearty Roman dishes like coda alla vaccinara (oxtail stew) or rigatoni alla pajata.

Choosing the best time to visit Rome ultimately depends on your personal preferences and priorities. If you value pleasant weather and vibrant cultural events, spring and autumn are ideal. For those who thrive in the energy of summer festivals or seek an intimate, crowd-free experience, summer and winter respectively offer their own rewards. Regardless of when you visit, Rome's timeless allure ensures that every season brings its own unique magic to the Eternal City. Planning your trip with the seasons in mind will not only enhance your experience but also allow you to connect with the city on a deeper, more personal level.

Essentials to Pack for Your Roman Adventure

Packing for a trip to Rome requires a thoughtful balance of practicality and preparation. The city's blend of ancient landmarks, bustling streets, and cultural treasures demands that travelers equip themselves for a variety of experiences, environments, and weather conditions. Whether you're visiting during the mild days of spring, the heat of summer, the crisp air of autumn, or the cooler winter months, your packing choices can significantly enhance your comfort and ability to enjoy the Eternal City to the fullest. By focusing on essentials that suit your itinerary, you can avoid overpacking and instead carry a curated selection of items that meet the demands of your Roman adventure.

Footwear is one of the most crucial elements of your packing list. Rome's cobblestone streets, uneven pavements, and historic sites require shoes that are both comfortable and durable. A pair of well-cushioned walking shoes or sneakers is indispensable for long days spent exploring landmarks like the Colosseum, the Roman Forum, or the Vatican. Opt for shoes with good arch support and solid soles to prevent fatigue and discomfort. Additionally, consider packing a pair of stylish yet comfortable flats or loafers for evenings out at Roman trattorias or piazzas, as they offer a more polished look while still accommodating the city's terrain. If you're visiting during the warmer months, breathable sandals with sturdy soles are a great alternative, but avoid flimsy flip-flops, as they provide little support and are unsuitable for extensive walking.

Layered clothing is key to navigating Rome's varied climate and cultural settings. Lightweight, breathable fabrics like cotton and linen are ideal for warmer months, as they keep you cool while allowing ease of movement. In spring and autumn, temperatures can vary throughout the day, so layering is essential. Pack a mix of short-sleeved tops and long-sleeved shirts, as well as a light jacket or cardigan that can be easily added or removed as temperatures shift. For winter visits, focus on warmth without bulk. A medium-weight coat, paired with thermal layers, is often sufficient, as Rome's winters are generally mild compared to other European cities. Accessories like scarves, gloves, and hats can be added for extra warmth without occupying too much luggage space.

When considering clothing, it's also important to account for Rome's cultural expectations and dress codes. Many of the city's most iconic sites, including St. Peter's Basilica and other churches, require modest attire for entry. This means covering shoulders and knees, so include at least one outfit that adheres to these guidelines. A maxi dress, long skirt, or lightweight pants combined with a shawl or cardigan can easily meet these requirements while keeping you comfortable during the warmer months. For men, long trousers and a collared shirt are appropriate and versatile options. Keeping these cultural norms in mind will help you avoid being turned away from sacred spaces and ensure a respectful visit.

A compact yet functional day bag is indispensable for carrying essentials as you explore the city. Choose a bag that is lightweight, secure, and easy to carry, such as a crossbody bag or a small backpack. The bag should have multiple compartments to organize items like maps, guidebooks, water bottles, and snacks. If you're planning to visit crowded areas like the Trevi Fountain or the Spanish Steps, opt for a bag with anti-theft features, such as lockable zippers or hidden pockets, to protect your belongings from pickpockets. Additionally, a foldable tote or reusable shopping bag is useful for carrying souvenirs or groceries from local markets like Campo de' Fiori or Testaccio.

Hydration is essential, especially during the warmer months, so pack a reusable water bottle to stay refreshed throughout the day. Rome's numerous public fountains, known as "nasoni," provide free and clean drinking water, making it easy to refill your bottle and reduce plastic waste. These fountains are scattered across the city, often near major landmarks, and their cool, refreshing water is a welcome relief during a day of sightseeing. A lightweight, collapsible water bottle is a great space-saving option for your bag.

Sun protection is another must for your Roman adventure, particularly if you're visiting during the spring or summer. The Mediterranean sun can be intense, so include a wide-brimmed hat or a baseball cap to shield your face from direct sunlight. Sunglasses with UV protection are also essential for preserving eye health and enhancing visibility during outdoor activities. A high-SPF sunscreen is a non-negotiable item, as it protects your skin from harmful rays during hours spent exploring open-air attractions like the Palatine Hill or the Appian Way. A small, travel-sized sunscreen can be conveniently stored in your day bag for reapplication throughout the day.

A small travel umbrella or a lightweight, packable rain jacket can be a lifesaver during unexpected rain showers, particularly in the autumn and winter months. Rome's weather can be unpredictable, and having protection from sudden downpours ensures that your plans won't be disrupted. A compact umbrella is easy to slip into your day bag, while a rain jacket can double as an extra layer of warmth when needed. If you're visiting during the wetter months, consider also packing water-resistant shoes to keep your feet dry as you navigate the city's streets.

Electronics are another area where thoughtful packing pays off. A universal travel adapter is essential for charging devices like phones, cameras, and laptops, as Italy uses a different plug type than many other countries. A portable power bank is also highly recommended, as long days of sightseeing can quickly drain your phone's battery, especially if you're using navigation apps or taking photos. Speaking of photos, a compact camera or a smartphone with a good camera is a must for capturing Rome's breathtaking scenery, from the grandeur of St. Peter's Square to the intricate details of Bernini's fountains. If you're an avid reader, consider bringing a lightweight e-reader loaded with travel guides, novels, or language resources to enjoy during downtime.

Travel documents and organizational tools should be packed with care. Ensure you have a valid passport, any necessary visas, and a printed or digital copy of your travel itinerary. Keep a photocopy of your passport in a separate location as a backup in case the original is lost or stolen. A small, zippered pouch or travel wallet is useful for organizing important items like boarding passes, train tickets, and museum reservation confirmations. If you're planning to use public transportation frequently, consider pre-purchasing a Roma Pass or a similar card to streamline access to buses, trams, and metro lines while also providing discounts at certain attractions.

For those interested in language and cultural immersion, a pocket phrasebook or a language app can enhance your experience. While many Romans speak English, learning a few basic Italian phrases can go a long way in establishing rapport and showing respect for the local culture. Simple greetings like "buongiorno" (good morning) and "grazie" (thank you) are always appreciated, and knowing how to ask for directions or order food in Italian can make your interactions more rewarding.

Finally, consider packing a small first-aid kit with essentials like adhesive bandages, pain relievers, and any prescription medications you require. Blisters are a common issue for travelers walking long distances, so include blister pads or moleskin to address any discomfort. Having these items on hand can save you the inconvenience of searching for a pharmacy in an unfamiliar city.

Packing for Rome is as much about preparation as it is about anticipation. By focusing on essentials that align with your itinerary, the season, and the city's unique demands, you can ensure a smooth and enjoyable trip. Thoughtful packing not only enhances your comfort but also allows you to fully immerse yourself in the wonders of Rome without unnecessary distractions. Whether you're strolling through the ancient ruins, savoring gelato by the Trevi Fountain, or marveling at the Sistine Chapel, having the right items at your disposal will make every moment of your Roman adventure all the more memorable.

CHAPTER 1: PLANNING YOUR TRIP TO ROME

Choosing the Right Area to Stay: Rome's Best Neighborhoods

Rome is a city of countless layers, each neighborhood offering a distinct personality, rhythm, and atmosphere. Choosing the right area to stay in is one of the most important decisions you'll make when planning your trip, as it will shape your experience of the Eternal City. Each district has its own unique charm, and where you choose to base yourself will depend on your preferences, budget, and the type of Roman adventure you want to have. Understanding the character of these neighborhoods will help you select the one that aligns with your vision, whether you're seeking history, nightlife, tranquility, or a mix of everything.

The historic center, or Centro Storico, is the heart of Rome and one of the most popular areas to stay. This neighborhood is a labyrinth of cobblestone streets, stunning piazzas, and centuries-old buildings, where every turn reveals a postcard-worthy view. Staying here means you'll be within walking distance of iconic landmarks like the Pantheon, Piazza Navona, and Campo de' Fiori. The atmosphere is lively, with a mix of locals and tourists filling the streets, especially in the evenings when the piazzas come alive with street performers and al fresco dining. Accommodations in the historic center tend to be boutique hotels or charming guesthouses housed in historic buildings, offering an authentic Roman experience. However, this central location comes at a premium price, and the area can be crowded during peak tourist seasons. If you love being in the midst of the action and want to soak in Rome's historic charm, this is the place for you.

Trastevere, located just across the Tiber River, is one of Rome's most enchanting neighborhoods. Known for its bohemian vibe and picturesque streets, Trastevere is a favorite among those seeking a more relaxed and authentic Roman experience. The area is characterized by its narrow, winding alleyways lined with ivy-draped buildings, vibrant street art, and traditional trattorias. Piazza Santa Maria in Trastevere serves as the neighborhood's focal point, where locals and visitors gather to enjoy the lively atmosphere. Trastevere is especially magical in the evenings when its trattorias and wine bars fill with laughter and conversation. While it's slightly removed from the hustle and bustle of the historic center, it's still within walking distance of major landmarks, or a short tram ride away. Accommodations here range from boutique hotels to cozy apartments, making it an excellent choice for couples, families, or solo travelers looking for a romantic yet laid-back base.

For those who prefer a more luxurious and elegant setting, the area around the Spanish Steps and Via Veneto is an excellent choice. This neighborhood is synonymous with sophistication, offering high-end shopping, luxury hotels, and fine dining. The Spanish Steps themselves are one of Rome's most famous landmarks, attracting visitors who want to climb to the top for stunning views of the city. Via Condotti, which runs from the steps, is a haven for designer boutiques, while Via Veneto is known for its glamorous history as a hub for celebrities during the Dolce Vita era. While this area caters to a more upscale clientele, it's also conveniently located, with easy access to Villa Borghese Park and other major attractions. If your idea of a perfect Roman holiday includes indulgence and style, staying near the Spanish Steps will not disappoint.

Monti, often described as one of Rome's hippest neighborhoods, is a fantastic option for travelers looking for a blend of history and contemporary culture. This area, nestled between the Colosseum and Piazza Venezia, is a treasure trove of hidden gems. Its narrow streets are lined with vintage shops, independent boutiques, and trendy cafes, giving it a distinctly youthful yet timeless vibe. Monti is a neighborhood where you can start your day exploring ancient ruins and end it sipping aperitifs at a local wine bar. The central location makes it easy to reach major landmarks, but Monti retains a more local feel compared to the bustling historic center. Accommodations here are varied, from boutique hotels to stylish rental apartments, making it a versatile choice for travelers who want to experience Rome's modern and historic sides simultaneously.

The Vatican area, including Prati, offers a quieter and more residential experience while still being close to some of Rome's most important landmarks. Staying here is particularly convenient for those planning to spend significant time exploring the Vatican Museums, St. Peter's Basilica, and the Sistine Chapel. The neighborhood of Prati, which borders the Vatican, is characterized by wide boulevards, elegant architecture, and a more subdued atmosphere. It's an excellent choice for families or travelers who prefer a peaceful retreat after a day of sightseeing. Prati is also known for its excellent shopping, particularly along Via Cola di Rienzo, and its vibrant restaurant scene, which includes some of the best gelaterias in the city. While it's slightly further from the historic center, the area is well-connected by public transportation, making it easy to access other parts of Rome.

If you're looking for a more off-the-beaten-path experience, consider staying in Testaccio. This neighborhood, once the heart of Rome's working-class community, is now a hub for food lovers and cultural enthusiasts. Testaccio is famous for its traditional Roman cuisine, with local trattorias serving dishes like cacio e pepe and carciofi alla romana. The Testaccio Market is a must-visit for foodies, offering everything from fresh produce to gourmet street food. The neighborhood also has a rich history, with landmarks like the Pyramid of Cestius and the Protestant Cemetery providing unique insights into Rome's past. Testaccio's nightlife scene is lively but less touristy than other areas, making it a great choice for those seeking an authentic Roman experience.

Accommodations here are often more affordable, ranging from budget-friendly hotels to cozy guesthouses.

Another alternative for travelers who value tranquility is the Aventine Hill. This residential neighborhood offers a serene escape from the city's bustling streets, with beautiful parks, quiet streets, and stunning views of Rome. The Orange Garden (Giardino degli Aranci) and the Aventine Keyhole are two of the area's highlights, providing moments of peace and breathtaking vistas. Staying on the Aventine Hill is ideal for couples or anyone seeking a romantic and relaxing setting. While it's less central than some other neighborhoods, the Aventine is still within walking distance of the Circus Maximus and other attractions, making it a hidden gem worth considering.

If proximity to Rome's central transportation hubs is a priority, the area around Termini Station might be a practical choice. This neighborhood, while not as picturesque as others, offers unparalleled convenience for travelers arriving by train or planning day trips to nearby destinations like Florence or Naples. Termini is also well-connected to Rome's metro and bus networks, making it easy to navigate the city. While the area has a reputation for being busier and more functional, it has seen a resurgence in recent years, with new restaurants, bars, and boutique hotels catering to modern travelers. For those on a budget, Termini offers some of the most affordable accommodations in the city, from hostels to mid-range hotels.

Choosing the right neighborhood to stay in is not just a logistical decision but an opportunity to shape your Roman experience. Each district offers its own unique perspective on the city, from the historic charm of the Centro Storico to the bohemian allure of Trastevere, the luxury of the Spanish Steps, and the authenticity of Testaccio. By considering your personal preferences, interests, and travel style, you can find the perfect base that allows you to connect with Rome in a way that feels most meaningful to you. Whether you're seeking history, culture, tranquility, or excitement, Rome's neighborhoods have something special to offer, ensuring that your stay is as unforgettable as the city itself.

The Ultimate Packing Checklist for Rome

Packing for a trip to Rome is an art in itself. The Eternal City, with its rich history, stunning architecture, and vibrant culture, requires a carefully curated assortment of essentials. Striking the right balance between practicality and preparedness is key, as Rome's diverse experiences—from exploring ancient ruins to dining at charming trattorias—demand a well-thought-out packing checklist. Whether you're visiting during the sweltering heat of summer or the brisk chill of winter, having the right items with you can make all the difference in ensuring a seamless and enjoyable adventure.

Footwear is the foundation of your packing strategy. Rome's streets, with their cobblestones and uneven surfaces, can be unforgiving on ill-prepared feet. A reliable pair of walking shoes is essential for navigating the city's endless treasures. Opt for comfortable, supportive footwear such as sneakers or walking sandals that can endure hours of exploration without causing discomfort. For evenings, when you may find yourself dining at a more upscale restaurant or strolling along the Tiber, pack a pair of stylish yet practical flats or loafers. Heels, while elegant, are best avoided due to the city's challenging terrain. If you're visiting during the wetter months, consider waterproof shoes or boots to ensure your feet stay dry as you traverse the city's historic streets.

Clothing choices should be guided by both the season and the cultural context of Rome. Lightweight, breathable fabrics like cotton and linen are ideal for Rome's hot summers, helping you stay cool while exploring outdoor landmarks like the Colosseum or the Roman Forum. Pack a mix of short-sleeved tops, sleeveless blouses, and shorts or loose-fitting skirts for daytime outings. During spring and autumn, layering is crucial, as temperatures can fluctuate throughout the day. A light sweater, cardigan, or jacket can be easily added or removed as needed. In winter, while Rome's temperatures rarely drop below freezing, a warm coat, scarf, and gloves are essential for comfort during outdoor activities. Always prioritize versatile pieces that can be mixed and matched to save space in your luggage.

Respect for Rome's cultural and religious customs should also influence your wardrobe choices. Many of the city's iconic attractions, such as St. Peter's Basilica and other churches, require modest attire for entry. Shoulders and knees must be covered, so include at least one outfit that adheres to these guidelines. Maxi dresses, long skirts, or lightweight pants paired with a shawl or scarf are excellent options for women, while men should pack long trousers and collared shirts for such occasions. These items not only ensure you meet entry requirements but also demonstrate respect for local traditions.

A well-organized day bag is indispensable for carrying your essentials while exploring Rome. Choose a bag that is both lightweight and secure, such as a crossbody bag or a small backpack. It should have multiple compartments to help you organize items like a reusable water bottle, guidebooks, and snacks. Anti-theft features, such as lockable zippers or hidden pockets, are highly recommended for peace of mind, especially in crowded areas like the Trevi Fountain or the Spanish Steps. A foldable tote or reusable shopping bag is also handy for carrying souvenirs or groceries from the city's bustling markets.

Staying hydrated is essential, particularly during the warmer months. Pack a reusable water bottle to take advantage of Rome's public fountains, or "nasoni," which provide free and clean drinking water throughout the city. These fountains are not only practical but also a unique feature of the Roman experience, adding a touch of charm to a basic necessity. A collapsible bottle is a convenient, space-saving option that fits easily into your day bag.

Sun protection is a non-negotiable addition to your packing list, especially if you're visiting Rome during its sunnier seasons. A wide-brimmed hat or a baseball cap can shield your face from the strong Mediterranean sun while adding a touch of style to your outfit. Sunglasses with UV protection are equally important for safeguarding your eyes and enhancing visibility during outdoor excursions. Don't forget to pack a high-SPF sunscreen to protect your skin during prolonged periods of sightseeing. A travel-sized sunscreen can be easily carried in your bag for reapplication throughout the day.

Unexpected weather is always a possibility, so be prepared with lightweight rain gear. A compact travel umbrella or a packable rain jacket can save the day during sudden downpours, particularly in the autumn and winter months. These items are easy to carry and ensure that your plans won't be derailed by unpredictable weather. If you're visiting during the rainy season, consider packing water-resistant footwear to keep your feet dry and comfortable.

Electronics play a vital role in modern travel, and Rome is no exception. A universal travel adapter is essential for charging your devices, as Italy uses a different plug type than many other countries. A portable power bank is another must-have, as long days of navigating the city and capturing photos can quickly drain your phone's battery. A smartphone with a good camera or a compact digital camera will help you document Rome's breathtaking sights, from the grandeur of St. Peter's Square to the intricate details of the Pantheon. If you plan to stay connected, ensure you have a local SIM card or an international data plan for seamless communication and navigation.

Organizational tools can make your trip more efficient and less stressful. Use a travel wallet or zippered pouch to keep important documents, such as your passport, travel itinerary, and museum reservations, in one place. It's also wise to carry a photocopy of your passport or store a digital copy on your phone as a backup. If you plan to use public transportation frequently, pre-purchase a Roma Pass or similar travel card to simplify your journeys and save time. These passes often include discounts on major attractions, making them a valuable addition to your travel kit.

First-aid essentials can save you from minor inconveniences during your trip. Pack a small kit with adhesive bandages, pain relievers, and any prescription medications you require. Blisters are a common issue for travelers exploring Rome on foot, so include blister pads or moleskin in your kit. Having these items on hand can prevent unnecessary detours to pharmacies and ensure you stay comfortable throughout your adventure.

For those seeking a deeper connection with Roman culture, consider packing tools for language and learning. A pocket phrasebook or language app can help you navigate interactions with locals and enhance your appreciation of Italian culture. While many Romans speak English, mastering a few basic phrases, such as "buongiorno" (good morning) or "grazie" (thank you), can create more meaningful connections and demonstrate respect for the local language.

Rome's culinary scene is legendary, and foodies may want to pack items that enhance their gastronomic experiences. A lightweight reusable utensil set or collapsible food container can be useful for enjoying street food or carrying leftovers from restaurants. If you're a coffee enthusiast, a small, portable coffee mug can add convenience to your morning espresso runs. These items not only enhance your experience but also support sustainable travel practices.

Packing for Rome is about anticipating the city's unique demands while leaving room for spontaneity. By focusing on versatile, functional items, you can ensure that you're prepared for everything from exploring ancient ruins to savoring gelato in charming piazzas. Thoughtful preparation allows you to fully immerse yourself in the magic of Rome without unnecessary distractions, making your journey as seamless and unforgettable as the city itself.

Budgeting for Your Trip: From Luxury to Budget-Friendly Travel

Planning a trip to Rome is as much about crafting a budget as it is about choosing what sights to see and neighborhoods to explore. The Eternal City offers experiences for every price point, from luxurious indulgences to wallet-conscious adventures, but creating a budget that aligns with your expectations is crucial for a smooth and enjoyable visit. Whether you're dreaming of a five-star stay overlooking Piazza Navona or a cozy guesthouse tucked into Trastevere's narrow streets, knowing how to approach costs for accommodation, dining, transportation, and entertainment will make all the difference. Rome's charm lies in its ability to cater to both extravagant and budget-conscious travelers, but the key is understanding how to allocate your funds wisely.

Accommodation will likely account for the largest portion of your budget, and Rome offers a range of options suitable for every traveler. At the high end, luxury hotels such as the Hassler Roma near the Spanish Steps or the Hotel de Russie on Via del Babuino provide an exceptional level of service, exquisite decor, and unparalleled locations. These hotels often include amenities like rooftop terraces, spas, and private gardens, making them ideal for travelers seeking a lavish experience. Prices for such accommodations can easily exceed €500 per night, especially during peak seasons, but the splurge often comes with the convenience of being steps away from major attractions.

For mid-range travelers, boutique hotels and well-reviewed guesthouses offer an excellent compromise between comfort and cost. These establishments, often housed in historic buildings, provide a more personal experience while maintaining proximity to key sites. Prices typically range from €100 to €250 per night, depending on the season and location. Neighborhoods like Monti, Trastevere, and Prati are particularly popular among mid-range travelers for their charm, local feel, and accessibility. If you're traveling as a group or staying for an extended period, consider renting an apartment through platforms like Airbnb or Vrbo. Apartments often provide additional space, kitchen facilities, and a more homely atmosphere, allowing you to save money on dining out by preparing some of your own meals.

Budget travelers can find plenty of affordable options without compromising on the experience. Hostels in Rome are plentiful, with many offering private rooms in addition to dormitory-style accommodations. The YellowSquare in Termini, for example, is a popular choice among younger travelers thanks to its vibrant social atmosphere and reasonable prices, which can start as low as €20 per night for a dorm bed. Alternatively, budget hotels and pensioni (family-run guesthouses) provide simple yet comfortable rooms, often with breakfast included. Staying slightly outside the city center, in areas like San Lorenzo or Testaccio, can also yield lower rates while still offering easy access to public transportation.

Dining in Rome is another area where your budget can vary significantly, but one of the city's greatest charms is its ability to provide unforgettable meals at almost any price point. High-end restaurants such as La Pergola at the Rome Cavalieri or Imàgo at the Hassler Roma offer Michelin-starred cuisine with breathtaking views, perfect for a special occasion. Expect to spend upwards of €150 per person for a multi-course meal with wine at these establishments. For a mid-range experience, trattorias and osterias are the backbone of Roman dining culture. Places like Roscioli in Campo de' Fiori or Da Enzo in Trastevere serve authentic dishes like carbonara, cacio e pepe, and saltimbocca at prices averaging €20 to €40 per person.

Budget-friendly dining in Rome is equally rewarding, with countless pizzerias, panini shops, and street food vendors offering delicious options for under €10. Supplì, a Roman specialty of fried rice balls filled with mozzarella, is a must-try snack that won't break the bank. Markets like Testaccio Market or Campo de' Fiori are excellent spots to enjoy fresh produce, cheeses, and meats at reasonable prices while soaking in the local atmosphere. Don't underestimate the appeal of Rome's coffee bars, where you can sip an espresso for as little as €1 while standing at the counter, just as the locals do.

Transportation in Rome is relatively affordable, making it easy to navigate the city without overspending. Public transportation, including buses, trams, and the metro, is the most cost-effective option. A single ticket costs €1.50 and is valid for 100 minutes, while a 24-hour pass is €7, and a 72-hour pass is €18, offering unlimited travel within those timeframes. The Roma Pass, available in 48-hour and 72-hour options, combines public transportation with discounted entry to museums and attractions, making it a great value for travelers planning to visit multiple sites. Taxis and ride-sharing services like Free Now are more expensive but can be useful for late-night journeys or areas not well-served by public transport. Walking, however, is often the best way to experience Rome's charm, as many of its attractions are clustered within a compact area.

When it comes to sightseeing, Rome offers plenty of opportunities to save money without sacrificing the quality of your experience. Key attractions like the Colosseum, Roman Forum, and Palatine Hill are often bundled into a single ticket, which costs €18 for adults. Booking tickets online in advance not only helps you skip the lines but also ensures availability, as these sites can sell out during busy periods. For budget travelers, consider visiting on the first Sunday of the month, when many state-run museums and archaeological sites offer free entry. Churches, including St. Peter's Basilica and the Pantheon, are generally free to enter, though some may charge a small fee for access to specific areas like the dome or crypt.

Rome is also a city where simply wandering the streets can be as rewarding as visiting its famous landmarks. Piazza Navona, the Trevi Fountain, and Campo de' Fiori are all free to enjoy and provide endless opportunities for people-watching and photography. Parks like Villa Borghese and the Orange Garden on the Aventine Hill offer tranquil escapes from the bustling city and are perfect for a picnic or a leisurely stroll. For a unique perspective, head to the Janiculum Hill or the Pincio Terrace, both of which provide stunning panoramic views of Rome at no cost.

Souvenirs and shopping can be another area where your budget plays a role. High-end shoppers will find luxury boutiques along Via Condotti and Via del Corso, while those seeking unique, budget-friendly items should explore local markets and artisan shops. The Campo de' Fiori market is a great place to pick up spices, olive oil, and other culinary delights, while the Porta Portese flea market in Trastevere offers everything from vintage clothing to antiques. Set a budget for souvenirs to avoid overspending, and remember that experiences often make the best keepsakes.

Budgeting for Rome also means accounting for hidden costs that might arise during your trip. Tipping, for example, is not as customary in Italy as it is in some other countries, but rounding up the bill or leaving a small amount of change is appreciated in restaurants and cafes. City taxes, which vary depending on the type of accommodation, are another expense to consider; these are usually charged per person, per night, and are collected at check-out. Travel insurance, while not mandatory, is a wise investment to cover unexpected situations such as medical emergencies or trip cancellations.

The beauty of Rome is that it offers something for everyone, regardless of budget. By carefully planning your spending across accommodation, dining, transportation, and activities, you can create a tailored experience that matches your financial goals. Whether you're savoring a gourmet meal overlooking the city or enjoying a simple gelato in a quiet piazza, the essence of Rome lies in its ability to enchant and inspire at every turn. Thoughtful budgeting allows you to immerse yourself fully in the magic of the Eternal City, ensuring that every euro spent adds value to your journey.

Navigating Rome's Transportation: Airports, Trains, and Public Transit

Arriving in Rome, a city brimming with history and vibrant energy, marks the beginning of an unforgettable journey. To fully embrace all the Eternal City has to offer, understanding its transportation system is essential. Rome offers an intricate web of options, ranging from its airports and train stations to its extensive public transit network. Whether you're flying into the city, traveling by rail, or navigating its bustling streets, having a clear grasp of Rome's transportation infrastructure will save time, reduce stress, and enhance your overall experience.

Rome is served by two main airports: Leonardo da Vinci International Airport, commonly referred to as Fiumicino (FCO), and Ciampino Airport (CIA). Fiumicino is the larger of the two and handles the majority of international flights, making it the primary gateway for visitors traveling from outside Italy. Located approximately 30 kilometers from the city center, Fiumicino offers several options for getting into Rome. The Leonardo Express train is one of the fastest and most convenient choices, taking just 32 minutes to connect the airport to Termini Station, Rome's central transportation hub. Tickets cost €14 and can be purchased online, at automated machines, or at kiosks within the airport.

Alternatively, regional trains operated by Trenitalia provide a cheaper option at €8 but take longer and stop at various stations along the way.

Taxis are another option for travelers arriving at Fiumicino. Official white taxis with a "Comune di Roma" sticker offer a flat rate of €50 to the city center, including luggage. While this might seem steep compared to public transit, it provides door-to-door service and can be more practical for those traveling with heavy luggage or arriving late at night. Private transfer services and rideshare apps like Free Now are also available but are typically more expensive than taxis. For budget-conscious travelers, shuttle buses operated by companies like Terravision and SIT Bus provide a cost-effective alternative, with tickets priced around €6 one-way.

Ciampino Airport, located about 15 kilometers from the city center, primarily serves low-cost carriers like Ryanair and Wizz Air. Due to its smaller size, navigating Ciampino is generally quicker and less overwhelming than Fiumicino. Transportation options from Ciampino to Rome include shuttle buses, which are the most popular choice among travelers. These buses connect the airport to Termini Station in approximately 40 minutes, with tickets costing between €5 and €7. Taxis from Ciampino to the city center operate at a flat rate of €31, making them a viable option for those seeking convenience. Unlike Fiumicino, Ciampino does not have a direct train connection, so buses or taxis are the primary means of transport.

For those arriving in Rome by train, Termini Station stands as the city's central hub and one of the busiest railway stations in Europe. Strategically located near the historic center, Termini connects Rome to other major Italian cities like Florence, Milan, and Naples, as well as international destinations. High-speed trains operated by Trenitalia (Frecciarossa and Frecciargento) and Italo offer fast and comfortable travel, with amenities like Wi-Fi and spacious seating. Termini itself is a bustling complex with shops, restaurants, and ticket counters, but it can feel overwhelming for first-time visitors. To avoid confusion, familiarize yourself with the station layout and keep an eye on the electronic departure boards, which display track numbers and departure times.

Other significant train stations in Rome include Tiburtina and Ostiense. Tiburtina serves as a secondary hub for high-speed Italo trains, while Ostiense is a key station for regional trains and those traveling to and from Fiumicino Airport via the FL1 line. Both stations are smaller and less chaotic than Termini, making them preferable for travelers seeking a quieter experience. Regardless of which station you use, purchasing train tickets in advance is highly recommended, especially for high-speed routes and during peak travel seasons. Tickets can be bought online through the Trenitalia or Italo websites, at automated machines, or at ticket counters within the stations.

Navigating Rome's public transportation network requires a basic understanding of its system, which includes buses, trams, and the metro. The metro, though limited compared to those in other major cities, is an efficient way to cover long distances quickly. Rome's metro consists of three lines: Line A (orange), Line B (blue), and Line C (green). Line A connects key tourist areas like the Spanish Steps, Vatican City, and Termini, while Line B serves landmarks such as the Colosseum and Circus Maximus. Line C is still under construction but currently operates in the city's southeastern suburbs. Metro tickets cost €1.50 for a single journey and are valid for 100 minutes, allowing transfers between buses and trams within that timeframe.

Buses and trams, operated by ATAC, provide extensive coverage of the city and reach areas not served by the metro. Popular bus routes include the 64, which connects Termini to Vatican City, and the 492, which passes through major landmarks like Piazza Navona and Campo de' Fiori. While buses are a convenient option, they can be crowded and subject to delays due to Rome's infamous traffic. Trams, on the other hand, are less crowded and offer a smoother ride, with routes like the Number 8 connecting Piazza Venezia to Trastevere. Tickets for buses and trams are the same as metro tickets and must be validated upon boarding.

Taxis in Rome can be a convenient option for short trips, but they are generally more expensive than public transportation. Official taxis are white with a "Comune di Roma" logo and can be hailed on the street or found at designated taxi stands. It's important to note that taxis in Rome do not routinely accept credit cards, so carrying cash is advisable. Rideshare apps like Free Now and Uber are also available but are often more expensive than traditional taxis.

One of the best ways to explore Rome is on foot. Many of the city's iconic landmarks are located within walking distance of each other, making it possible to experience much of Rome's charm without relying on transportation. Walking allows you to discover hidden gems, like quaint alleyways and tucked-away piazzas, that you might otherwise miss. However, be prepared for uneven cobblestone streets and occasional steep inclines, especially in historic areas like the Aventine Hill.

For travelers planning to use public transportation frequently, purchasing a travel pass can offer significant savings and convenience. Options include the 24-hour (€7), 48-hour (€12.50), or 72-hour (€18) passes, as well as the weekly pass (€24). These passes provide unlimited travel on buses, trams, and the metro within their respective timeframes. The Roma Pass, available in 48-hour (€32) and 72-hour (€52) versions, combines unlimited public transportation with discounted entry to museums and archaeological sites, making it an excellent value for culture-focused travelers.

Rome's transportation system, while not without its quirks and challenges, offers a variety of options to suit every type of traveler. Whether you're arriving by air, rail, or simply navigating the city's maze-like streets, understanding how to move efficiently will make your trip far more enjoyable. By combining public transit, taxis, and walking, you can experience the best of Rome while minimizing stress and maximizing your time in this extraordinary city.

Safety and Travel Tips: Staying Safe in a Busy City

Rome is a city that thrives on its energy—its bustling piazzas, vibrant streets, and lively markets are as much a part of its identity as its ancient ruins and Renaissance art. However, as with any major tourist destination, navigating a city as dynamic as Rome requires a certain level of awareness and preparation to ensure you stay safe and make the most of your time exploring. From managing pickpockets in crowded areas to understanding local customs and emergency resources, being informed can help you avoid common mishaps and fully enjoy the Eternal City.

Pickpockets are perhaps the most common concern for visitors to Rome, and their tactics are often subtle and well-practiced. Crowded attractions like the Colosseum, Trevi Fountain, and Vatican City are prime hotspots for pickpockets, as are public transportation hubs such as Termini Station or the metro during rush hours. To minimize your risk, consider using an anti-theft bag with lockable zippers or hidden compartments. Wearing a crossbody bag and keeping it in front of you, rather than on your back or side, makes it harder for potential thieves to access your belongings. Avoid carrying large amounts of cash; opt instead for a combination of cash and credit cards, and split these between different pockets or bags so you're not left stranded in case of theft. A money belt worn discreetly under your clothing is an effective way to store passports and other important documents.

While you're enjoying the vibrant atmosphere of Rome's streets, be particularly vigilant in situations that involve distractions, as these are often orchestrated by pickpockets.

Common tactics include someone dropping coins or spilling a drink nearby to divert your attention while an accomplice targets your bag. Another frequent ruse involves individuals pretending to offer you something for free, such as a bracelet or flower, only to demand payment once you've accepted. Politely but firmly decline such offers and keep walking. Awareness is your best defense—if something feels off, trust your instincts and remove yourself from the situation.

Aside from pickpocketing, scams targeting tourists are another issue to watch out for. Fake tour guides or ticket sellers may approach you near major attractions, offering expedited entry or discounted access. Always purchase tickets for attractions from official websites or authorized vendors to avoid being overcharged or denied entry. Similarly, be cautious of overly friendly strangers who claim to be locals eager to show you around. While there are certainly genuine acts of kindness, this can sometimes be a pretext for leading you into a scam or pressuring you into spending money at specific businesses.

Crossing the street in Rome can feel like an adventure in itself. Traffic in the city is famously chaotic, with cars, scooters, and buses weaving through narrow streets at what seems like breakneck speed. Pedestrian crossings exist, but drivers don't always stop unless you assertively step into the crosswalk. Make eye contact with approaching drivers to ensure they see you, and cross confidently but cautiously. If you're unsure, wait for a group of locals to cross and follow their lead—Romans navigate their city's traffic with practiced ease and can often provide a sense of safety in numbers.

At night, Rome transforms into a magical landscape of illuminated monuments and lively piazzas, but it's important to stay aware of your surroundings, especially in quieter areas. Stick to well-lit streets and avoid walking alone in isolated neighborhoods. Areas like Trastevere and Campo de' Fiori are popular for their nightlife but can become rowdy late into the evening. If you're out enjoying Rome's vibrant bar scene, keep an eye on your drink to avoid issues with spiking, and always have a plan for getting back to your accommodation safely. Taxis are a reliable option for late-night travel, but make sure to use official white taxis with the "Comune di Roma" logo or a trusted rideshare service.

Staying safe in Rome also involves being mindful of your physical well-being. The city's cobblestone streets, uneven pavements, and steep hills can be challenging, especially for those unaccustomed to walking long distances. Wear comfortable, sturdy shoes to reduce the risk of tripping or injuring yourself. During the summer months, the Mediterranean sun can be intense, so stay hydrated by carrying a refillable water bottle and taking advantage of Rome's public fountains, or "nasoni," which provide free drinking water throughout the city. Applying sunscreen and wearing a hat can also protect you from the heat, particularly when exploring open-air landmarks like the Roman Forum or Palatine Hill.

Emergency preparedness is another essential aspect of staying safe while traveling in Rome. Familiarize yourself with the local emergency numbers: 112 is the general emergency line in Italy, while 118 is specifically for medical emergencies. Pharmacies, marked with a green cross, are widely available and can assist with minor medical needs, such as over-the-counter medications or first aid supplies. If you require medical attention, many pharmacies can also direct you to nearby clinics or hospitals. For non-emergency issues, your hotel staff or host is often an invaluable resource for guidance and assistance.

Understanding local customs and etiquette can also enhance your safety and experience in Rome. While Romans are generally warm and welcoming, certain behaviors can inadvertently cause offense or draw unwanted attention. Dress modestly when visiting religious sites, ensuring your shoulders and knees are covered. Be respectful when taking photos—asking permission before photographing people or their property is a simple courtesy that goes a long way. Additionally, avoid loud or disruptive behavior, especially in residential areas, as this can be seen as disrespectful.

Rome's public transportation system, while efficient, can be another area where caution is necessary. The metro and buses can become crowded, particularly during peak hours, making them a target for pickpockets. Keep your belongings close and avoid placing bags on the seat next to you, as this can invite attention. If you're using the metro late at night, try to travel with others and remain aware of your surroundings. When purchasing tickets, use official ATAC vending machines or authorized sellers to avoid counterfeit tickets, which can result in fines if discovered during inspections.

Despite the challenges, Rome remains one of the most enchanting cities in the world, and a little preparation can go a long way in ensuring a safe and enjoyable visit. By staying vigilant, respecting local customs, and being mindful of your surroundings, you can immerse yourself in the city's magic without unnecessary stress. From the awe-inspiring beauty of the Sistine Chapel to the lively charm of Piazza Navona, Rome invites you to explore its treasures with confidence and curiosity, creating memories that will last a lifetime.

CHAPTER 2: MUST-SEE LANDMARKS IN ROME

The Colosseum: A Step Back in Time

The Colosseum, an enduring symbol of Rome's grandeur and history, stands as one of the most magnificent structures of the ancient world. Known formally as the Flavian Amphitheatre, it is a testament to the ingenuity of Roman engineering and the cultural complexity of an empire that expanded across continents. Walking through its colossal arches and gazing upon its towering walls, visitors are transported back nearly two thousand years to an era when this architectural marvel served as the epicenter of public entertainment, political displays, and social gatherings. To truly appreciate its significance, understanding the Colosseum's history, design, purpose, and modern-day preservation is essential.

Construction of the Colosseum began in 72 AD under Emperor Vespasian of the Flavian dynasty and was completed in 80 AD by his son, Titus. Built on the site of Nero's Golden House—the Domus Aurea—it was a deliberate effort by the Flavian emperors to erase the memory of Nero's opulence and return the land to the Roman people. The amphitheater was funded through the spoils of the Jewish-Roman War and symbolized the strength and prosperity of the empire. It could accommodate an astonishing 50,000 to 80,000 spectators, making it the largest amphitheater ever constructed. The decision to construct such a monumental public space was as much a political move as it was a testament to engineering brilliance; it solidified the emperor's image as a leader for the people.

The amphitheater's design is a masterpiece of Roman engineering, showcasing a combination of durability, functionality, and aesthetic appeal. Made primarily of travertine, tuff, and concrete, the Colosseum's elliptical shape ensured optimal visibility for spectators seated throughout its tiers. Its exterior facade features four stories of arches, with the first three levels adorned by columns in Doric, Ionic, and Corinthian styles, respectively. The top level, known as the attic, was punctuated with small windows and originally supported a velarium, a massive retractable awning that provided shade for the audience. This complex system of ropes and pulleys, operated by sailors from the Roman Navy, demonstrated the Romans' advanced understanding of mechanics.

Perhaps the most impressive aspect of the Colosseum's design lies beneath the arena floor. The hypogeum, an intricate underground network of tunnels and chambers, housed gladiators, wild animals, and stage machinery. Elevators and trapdoors allowed animals and fighters to appear suddenly in the arena, adding an element of surprise to the spectacles. The floor itself, made of wooden planks covered with sand, was designed to absorb blood and other fluids during combat. The hypogeum's complexity reveals the extent to which the Romans went to create elaborate and thrilling performances, ensuring the Colosseum's reputation as the ultimate venue for entertainment.

The spectacles held within the Colosseum were as varied as they were spectacular, reflecting the tastes and values of Roman society. Gladiatorial combat, the most famous of these events, pitted trained fighters against one another in battles that ranged from displays of skill to life-or-death struggles. These gladiators, often slaves or prisoners of war, could earn fame and, in rare cases, freedom through their prowess in the arena. Beyond gladiatorial games, the Colosseum hosted venationes, or animal hunts, where exotic creatures from across the empire—lions, elephants, and tigers—were showcased and killed in carefully staged hunts. Public executions were another grim feature, often dramatized to resemble mythological tales. The naumachiae, or mock naval battles, were particularly elaborate; the arena was flooded with water to simulate seas, allowing ships to engage in combat. These events were not merely entertainment but served as displays of imperial power, wealth, and Rome's dominance over nature and its enemies.

The Colosseum was more than a venue for violence and spectacle; it was also a tool of political propaganda. Emperors used the games to curry favor with the populace, offering free entry and food during events to project an image of generosity and benevolence. The amphitheater served as a stage for reinforcing Roman ideals of valor, discipline, and the superiority of Roman civilization. The audience, drawn from all social classes, was seated according to a strict hierarchy, with the emperor and senators occupying the best seats near the arena, while women and the poor were relegated to the upper tiers. This arrangement reflected and reinforced the social order of Roman society, making the Colosseum a microcosm of the empire itself.

Over the centuries, the Colosseum underwent significant changes, mirroring the shifting fortunes of Rome. After the decline of the Western Roman Empire in the 5th century, the amphitheater fell into disuse and was gradually repurposed. Its stone and metal were stripped for use in other buildings, including St. Peter's Basilica and palaces across the city. By the Middle Ages, it had become a fortress for local families, and later, a site of religious significance. In the 18th century, the Catholic Church consecrated the Colosseum as a sacred site commemorating Christian martyrs who were believed to have been executed there, though the historical accuracy of these claims remains debated.

Efforts to preserve the Colosseum began in earnest during the 19th century, as it was recognized as a cultural treasure of immense historical value. Today, the Colosseum is a UNESCO World Heritage Site and one of the New Seven Wonders of the World, drawing millions of visitors each year. Ongoing restoration projects aim to stabilize its structure and protect it from environmental damage, including pollution and seismic activity. Modern technology, such as 3D scanning and virtual reconstructions, has further enhanced our understanding of the Colosseum's original design and function.

Visiting the Colosseum offers a chance to connect with history in a profoundly personal way. Standing in the arena, where gladiators once fought for their lives, or walking through the hypogeum, where animals waited in the shadows, brings the past to life in vivid detail. Guided tours provide invaluable insights into the history and architecture of the amphitheater, while self-guided explorations allow visitors to linger in its arches and corridors at their own pace. For a truly unforgettable experience, consider visiting at sunrise or sunset, when the soft light bathes the Colosseum in a golden glow, creating an atmosphere that feels almost timeless.

As you explore the Colosseum, it's impossible not to reflect on the paradox it represents: a place of both incredible architectural achievement and brutal human spectacle. It is a reminder of the heights and depths of human civilization, of the ingenuity that built such a structure and the darker impulses it served. Yet, it is also a testament to Rome's enduring legacy, a symbol of a city that continues to captivate and inspire the world.

The Colosseum remains one of the most compelling reasons to visit Rome, offering a window into the grandeur and complexity of the ancient world. Its massive arches and intricate details tell the story of an empire at its zenith, while its enduring presence speaks to the resilience of human creativity. Whether you're drawn to its history, architecture, or cultural significance, the Colosseum invites you to take a step back in time and experience the heart of ancient Rome.

The Roman Forum and Palatine Hill

The Roman Forum and Palatine Hill stand at the heart of ancient Rome, a sprawling testament to the city's grandeur, political power, and cultural influence. Walking through this historic area is like stepping into the pages of history, where ruins of temples, basilicas, and triumphal arches whisper stories of emperors, senators, and citizens who shaped the Roman Empire. No visit to Rome is complete without exploring this fascinating archaeological site, which offers a glimpse into the world that once dominated the Mediterranean and beyond.

Nestled in the valley between the Capitoline and Palatine Hills, the Roman Forum was the bustling epicenter of political, religious, and social life in ancient Rome. Originally a marshland, it was drained in the 7th century BCE to create a central area where the city's most important public and ceremonial buildings could be constructed. Over the centuries, the Forum evolved into a vibrant space where triumphal processions, elections, public speeches, and criminal trials took place. It was here that the fate of the empire was debated and decided, making it one of the most significant places in Roman history.

The first thing that strikes you when entering the Roman Forum is the sheer scale of the ruins. The site is a sprawling maze of columns, arches, and foundations that once supported some of the most magnificent structures of antiquity. One of the most iconic landmarks is the Arch of Titus, a triumphal arch that commemorates Emperor Titus's victory in the Jewish-Roman War and the sacking of Jerusalem in 70 CE. The reliefs carved into the arch depict Roman soldiers carrying spoils from the Jewish Temple, including the famed Menorah, providing a vivid snapshot of history frozen in stone.

Nearby, the Temple of Saturn stands as one of the oldest temples in the Forum, its towering columns a reminder of

Rome's early dedication to the god of agriculture and wealth. The temple also served as the state treasury, where the spoils of war and public funds were stored. Further along, the Basilica of Maxentius and Constantine dominates the landscape with its enormous arches. Originally constructed as a civic building, this basilica was the largest structure in the Forum and showcased Rome's architectural prowess with its innovative use of concrete and vaulted ceilings.

The Curia, or Senate House, is another must-see structure within the Forum. Rebuilt several times over the centuries, the Curia was where the Roman Senate met to deliberate on matters of state. Its plain exterior contrasts sharply with the grandeur of other buildings in the Forum, reflecting its function as a place of serious political discourse. Inside, the marble floors and tiered seating evoke a sense of the power and responsibility that rested within these walls. Standing here, you can almost hear the echoes of senators debating laws, alliances, and the future of the empire.

Not far from the Curia lies the Rostra, the platform from which orators addressed the public. It was here that some of Rome's most famous speeches were delivered, including those by Cicero and Julius Caesar. The Rostra was adorned with the prows of captured enemy ships, a symbol of Rome's naval dominance. Imagine the crowds gathered to hear announcements, debates, and declarations that would shape their lives, their voices rising and falling with the passions of the speakers.

Palatine Hill, rising above the Forum, holds a special place in Roman mythology and history. According to legend, this is where Romulus founded the city of Rome after defeating his twin brother Remus in a dispute over where to establish their settlement. Archaeological evidence suggests that the hill was one of the earliest inhabited areas of Rome, dating back to the 10th century BCE. Over time, the Palatine became the preferred residential area for Rome's elite, including emperors who built opulent palaces overlooking the Forum.

One of the most striking features of the Palatine is the Domus Augustana, the sprawling palace complex of Emperor Augustus. This residence not only served as a private home but also as a political statement, embodying the power and stability of the Augustan era. The palace included elaborate gardens, courtyards, and frescoed rooms, many of which still display traces of their original decoration. Nearby, the House of Livia, believed to be the home of Augustus's wife, offers a glimpse into the domestic life of Rome's first imperial family.

The Palatine Hill also boasts breathtaking views of the Forum, the Colosseum, and the surrounding city. From the Farnese Gardens, a Renaissance addition to the site, visitors can enjoy a panoramic perspective that ties together Rome's ancient and modern landscapes. The gardens themselves are a peaceful retreat, with neatly arranged flowerbeds, fountains, and shaded pathways that provide a welcome respite from the bustling streets below.

Exploring the Roman Forum and Palatine Hill requires time and a sense of curiosity. The site is vast, and each ruin holds a story waiting to be discovered. To make the most of your visit, consider joining a guided tour or renting an audio guide, as the historical significance of many structures can be overlooked without proper context. Maps and signage are helpful, but the insights of an expert can bring the ruins to life, revealing the layers of history and culture that shaped this remarkable area.

Practical considerations are also essential for a comfortable visit. The Roman Forum and Palatine Hill are mostly outdoors, so wear comfortable shoes and be prepared for uneven terrain, as the ancient pathways can be challenging to navigate. Bring water, especially during the hotter months, as the site offers limited shade. Early mornings or late afternoons are the best times to visit, not only to avoid crowds but also to enjoy the softer light that enhances the beauty of the ruins.

The preservation and restoration of the Roman Forum and Palatine Hill are ongoing efforts, reflecting the importance of these sites as cultural and historical treasures. Archaeologists and historians continue to uncover new information about the area, deepening our understanding of ancient Rome. Visiting these sites is not only an opportunity to connect with the past but also a chance to appreciate the work being done to ensure that future generations can experience this extraordinary legacy.

The Roman Forum and Palatine Hill are more than just ruins; they are a portal to a world that shaped the foundations of Western civilization. Walking through these ancient spaces, you can feel the weight of history beneath your feet and the echoes of a society that, though long gone, continues to influence our world today. The grandeur, ambition, and ingenuity of ancient Rome are etched into every column and arch, inviting us to reflect on the enduring legacy of a civilization that once ruled the known world.

St. Peter's Basilica: A Spiritual Masterpiece

St. Peter's Basilica, an awe-inspiring testament to faith, art, and architecture, is one of the most iconic landmarks in the world. Located in Vatican City, this monumental structure is not only the spiritual epicenter of Catholicism but also a breathtaking masterpiece of Renaissance and Baroque design. Every inch of the basilica tells a story—of devotion, ambition, and the relentless pursuit of beauty. As you step into its sacred space, you are enveloped in centuries of history, religious significance, and artistic genius, making it a must-visit destination for travelers and pilgrims alike.

The origins of St. Peter's Basilica trace back to the early days of Christianity. According to tradition, it is built on the site where Saint Peter, one of Jesus Christ's apostles and the first pope, was martyred and buried. In 64 AD, during the reign of Emperor Nero, Saint Peter was crucified upside down in the Circus of Nero, an ancient chariot-racing stadium located on the Vatican Hill. His burial site quickly became a place of veneration for early Christians, who risked persecution to honor their leader. By the early 4th century, Emperor Constantine, the first Roman emperor to convert to Christianity, ordered the construction of a basilica over Saint Peter's tomb. This original structure, known as Old St. Peter's Basilica, stood for over a thousand years before it was eventually replaced by the current basilica.

The construction of the modern St. Peter's Basilica began in 1506 under the patronage of Pope Julius II and was completed in 1626 during the papacy of Urban VIII. Over a century in the making, the basilica brought together some of the greatest minds of the Renaissance and Baroque periods, including Bramante, Michelangelo, Bernini, and Raphael. Each architect and artist left their indelible mark on the structure, contributing to its grandeur and complexity. The final result is a harmonious blend of styles that reflect the evolving artistic and architectural trends of the time.

Approaching St. Peter's Basilica, visitors are greeted by the vast expanse of St. Peter's Square, designed by Gian Lorenzo Bernini in the 17th century. The elliptical square, bordered by two sweeping colonnades of Doric columns, symbolizes the open arms of the Church welcoming the faithful. At the center of the square stands an ancient Egyptian obelisk, brought to Rome by Emperor Caligula in 37 AD and later moved to its current location by Pope Sixtus V. Two fountains, one by Bernini and the other by Carlo Maderno, complete the square's symmetrical design, creating a sense of balance and serenity. The square is not only a gathering place for pilgrims and tourists but also the site of important papal ceremonies, such as Easter and Christmas blessings.

As you enter the basilica, the sheer scale of the interior is overwhelming. The nave, flanked by massive Corinthian columns, stretches toward the high altar, drawing your gaze upward to the soaring dome designed by Michelangelo. At 136 meters tall and 42 meters in diameter, the dome is one of the largest in the world and a defining feature of the Roman skyline. Michelangelo, who took over the project in 1547, envisioned the dome as a symbol of heaven, its intricate mosaics and gilded details adding to the celestial effect. Standing beneath it, you can't help but feel a sense of awe and wonder, as if the space itself is reaching toward the divine.

The high altar, or Baldacchino, is another masterpiece within the basilica. Designed by Bernini, this towering bronze canopy stands over the tomb of Saint Peter, emphasizing the connection between the present and the past, between the Church and its origins. The twisted Solomonic columns of the Baldacchino are adorned with intricate details, including bees and laurel leaves, symbols of the Barberini family to which Pope Urban VIII belonged. The altar is reserved for the pope, highlighting its significance as the spiritual heart of the Catholic Church.

One of the most famous works of art in St. Peter's Basilica is Michelangelo's Pietà, a sculpture that depicts the Virgin Mary cradling the lifeless body of Jesus after his crucifixion. Created when Michelangelo was only 24 years old, the Pietà is a stunning example of Renaissance sculpture, combining technical perfection with profound emotional depth. The delicacy of Mary's expression and the lifelike rendering of Christ's body evoke a sense of both sorrow and serenity, making it one of the most moving pieces of religious art ever created. The sculpture is displayed in a chapel to the right of the entrance, protected by a glass barrier after a vandalism incident in 1972.

Throughout the basilica, chapels and altars dedicated to various saints and religious figures invite visitors to pause and reflect. The Chapel of the Blessed Sacrament, designed by Carlo Maderno and later enhanced by Bernini, is a particularly serene space for prayer and contemplation. The ornate decoration, featuring gilded angels and marble inlays, creates an atmosphere of reverence and intimacy. Another notable feature is the statue of Saint Peter Enthroned, a bronze sculpture believed to date back to the 13th century. Pilgrims often touch or kiss the foot of the statue as a gesture of devotion, a tradition that has worn the metal smooth over the centuries.

Climbing to the dome of St. Peter's Basilica is an unforgettable experience that offers panoramic views of Vatican City and Rome. The ascent includes a combination of elevators and narrow, winding staircases, providing a closer look at the dome's intricate mosaics along the way. At the top, visitors are rewarded with a breathtaking vista that stretches from the Tiber River to the distant hills, a reminder of Rome's enduring beauty and significance. The climb requires a bit of effort, but the view is well worth it, offering a perspective that few places in the world can match.

The crypt beneath the basilica, known as the Vatican Grottoes, houses the tombs of numerous popes, including Saint Peter himself. This sacred space is a place of quiet reflection, where visitors can pay their respects to the leaders of the Church who have shaped its history. The simplicity of Saint Peter's tomb contrasts with the grandeur above, serving as a poignant reminder of the humility and sacrifice that lie at the core of the Christian faith.

Visiting St. Peter's Basilica requires some practical preparation. Admission to the basilica is free, but there is a fee for climbing the dome or accessing the Vatican Grottoes. Modest attire is required, with shoulders and knees covered, as a sign of respect for the sacred space. Arriving early in the morning or late in the afternoon can help you avoid the largest crowds, especially during peak tourist seasons. Guided tours and audio guides are available for those who wish to gain deeper insights into the basilica's history and art.

Preserving St. Peter's Basilica is an ongoing effort, as time, pollution, and the constant flow of visitors take their toll on the structure. Restoration projects, funded by both the Church and private donors, ensure that future generations can continue to marvel at this spiritual and artistic masterpiece. Advances in technology, such as laser scanning and 3D modeling, have allowed for more precise conservation techniques, helping to protect the basilica's intricate details from further damage.

St. Peter's Basilica is more than just a building; it is a symbol of faith, creativity, and the enduring human spirit. Its walls have witnessed the ebb and flow of history, from the rise of Christianity to the challenges of the modern world. Whether you visit as a pilgrim seeking spiritual solace or as a traveler drawn by its beauty and significance, the basilica offers an experience that transcends time and place. Standing within its hallowed halls, you are reminded of the power of belief and the extraordinary heights humanity can achieve in its pursuit of the divine.

The Vatican Museums and the Sistine Chapel

The Vatican Museums and the Sistine Chapel represent one of the richest collections of art and history in the world, attracting millions of visitors each year to marvel at their treasures. Located within the walls of Vatican City, these institutions are a testament to the Catholic Church's centuries-long patronage of the arts and its role in preserving some of humanity's greatest achievements. Walking through these halls is not simply a visit to a museum; it is a journey through time, culture, and spirituality, where every corner reveals masterpieces that have shaped the course of art and history. To fully appreciate this extraordinary experience, understanding the history, layout, and highlights of the Vatican Museums and Sistine Chapel is essential.

The origins of the Vatican Museums date back to 1506, when Pope Julius II acquired the Laocoön and His Sons, an ancient Greek sculpture unearthed in a vineyard near Rome. Recognizing its artistic and cultural significance, Julius II displayed the statue in the Belvedere Courtyard of the Vatican, effectively laying the foundation for what would become one of the most extensive art collections in the world. Over the centuries, successive popes continued to expand the collection, commissioning works from renowned artists and acquiring artifacts from across the globe. Today, the Vatican Museums consist of 54 galleries, or "salles," spanning nearly seven kilometers of corridors and rooms, making it one of the largest museum complexes in existence.

Navigating the Vatican Museums can be an overwhelming experience due to their sheer size and the density of their exhibits. The museums are organized into several distinct sections, each dedicated to different periods, styles, or themes. The Egyptian Museum houses artifacts from ancient Egypt, including mummies, sarcophagi, and statues, offering a glimpse into one of the world's earliest civilizations. Nearby, the Etruscan Museum showcases artifacts from the pre-Roman Etruscan civilization, including intricately decorated vases, jewelry, and funerary items. These collections highlight the Vatican's commitment to preserving the heritage of cultures far beyond its own.

The Gallery of Maps is one of the most visually captivating sections of the Vatican Museums. Stretching 120 meters, the gallery features 40 frescoed maps of Italy and its regions, created between 1580 and 1585 under the direction of Pope

Gregory XIII. The maps are not only remarkable for their artistic beauty but also for their historical and geographical significance, providing a snapshot of the world as it was understood in the late 16th century. Walking through this gilded corridor, with its ornate ceiling and vibrant frescoes, feels like stepping into a grand cartographic tapestry.

Another highlight of the Vatican Museums is the Raphael Rooms, a suite of four papal apartments adorned with frescoes by Raphael and his workshop. Commissioned by Pope Julius II in the early 16th century, these rooms are a celebration of Renaissance art and philosophy. The most famous of the frescoes is The School of Athens, located in the Stanza della Segnatura. This masterpiece depicts an assembly of great philosophers, scientists, and thinkers, including Plato, Aristotle, Socrates, and Pythagoras, portrayed with lifelike expressions and dynamic poses. Raphael's use of perspective and his ability to convey intellectual depth through artistic composition make this work a cornerstone of Western art.

The Vatican Museums are also home to the Pinacoteca, or Picture Gallery, which houses an impressive collection of paintings from the 12th to the 19th centuries. Works by masters such as Leonardo da Vinci, Caravaggio, and Titian are displayed here, offering visitors a chance to see some of the most celebrated pieces of European art. One of the standout works is Raphael's Transfiguration, a luminous depiction of the biblical event that is often regarded as his final and greatest painting. The Pinacoteca provides a more intimate viewing experience compared to the more crowded sections of the museums, allowing art enthusiasts to appreciate these masterpieces in relative tranquility.

No visit to the Vatican Museums would be complete without experiencing the Sistine Chapel, the crowning jewel of Vatican City and arguably one of the most famous artistic achievements in history. As you enter this sacred space, the first thing that strikes you is the ceiling, an awe-inspiring fresco painted by Michelangelo between 1508 and 1512. Commissioned by Pope Julius II, the ceiling depicts scenes from the Book of Genesis, including the iconic Creation of Adam, where God and Adam's fingertips nearly touch, symbolizing the spark of divine creation. Michelangelo's use of vibrant colors, dynamic figures, and innovative compositions revolutionized fresco painting and set a new standard for artistic excellence.

The Sistine Chapel's Last Judgment, painted by Michelangelo between 1536 and 1541, adorns the altar wall and is equally breathtaking. This monumental fresco portrays the Second Coming of Christ and the final judgment of souls, with a dramatic interplay of light and shadow that conveys both hope and terror. The figures, rendered with anatomical precision, seem to leap off the wall, their expressions and gestures capturing the emotional intensity of the scene. Michelangelo's work in the Sistine Chapel is not merely a display of technical mastery but also a profound exploration of theological and existential themes, making it a deeply moving experience for viewers.

The Sistine Chapel is not only an artistic marvel but also a place of great religious significance. It serves as the site of the papal conclave, the process by which a new pope is elected. During the conclave, cardinals from around the world gather in the chapel to cast their votes in secrecy, a tradition that underscores the chapel's role as the spiritual heart of the Catholic Church. The Sistine Chapel's connection to both art and faith creates a unique atmosphere that resonates with visitors, whether they come as pilgrims or art lovers.

Visiting the Vatican Museums and Sistine Chapel requires careful planning to make the most of your experience. Tickets should be purchased in advance, as the museums are among the most popular attractions in the world and lines can be exceedingly long. Guided tours and audio guides are highly recommended, as they provide valuable context and insights that enhance your understanding of the exhibits. Early morning or late afternoon visits are ideal for avoiding the largest crowds, allowing you to explore the galleries at a more leisurely pace.

Dress codes are strictly enforced within Vatican City, so be sure to wear modest attire that covers your shoulders and knees. Comfortable shoes are also essential, as the museums' extensive layout involves a considerable amount of walking. Photography is allowed in most areas of the Vatican Museums but is strictly prohibited in the Sistine Chapel, so take the opportunity to fully immerse yourself in the beauty of the frescoes without distractions.

Preservation of the Vatican Museums and Sistine Chapel is an ongoing challenge, given the immense number of visitors and the delicate nature of the artworks. Climate control systems, careful monitoring of light exposure, and regular restoration efforts are all part of the Vatican's efforts to protect these treasures for future generations. Visitors play a role in this preservation by respecting the rules and guidelines in place, ensuring that these extraordinary works of art remain accessible to all.

The Vatican Museums and Sistine Chapel are more than just a collection of art and artifacts; they are a celebration of human creativity, spirituality, and the enduring quest for beauty and meaning. Each gallery, sculpture, and fresco tells a story that transcends time and place, inviting us to reflect on the richness of our shared heritage. As you walk through these hallowed halls, you become part of a continuum that stretches back thousands of years, connecting you to the artists, patrons, and visionaries who shaped the world as we know it. It is an experience that leaves an indelible impression, inspiring wonder and reverence in equal measure.

The Pantheon: Ancient Architecture at Its Finest

The Pantheon, a marvel of ancient engineering and design, stands as one of the best-preserved relics of Rome's imperial past. Its massive dome, still the largest unreinforced concrete dome in the world, has captivated architects, historians, and visitors for nearly two millennia. Situated in the bustling Piazza della Rotonda, the Pantheon is not only an architectural masterpiece but also a symbol of the ingenuity and ambition of Roman civilization. Its name, derived from the Greek words pan (all) and theos (gods), reveals its original purpose as a temple dedicated to all the gods of pagan Rome. Today, it serves as a testament to the enduring legacy of ancient Rome, combining technical brilliance with timeless elegance.

The Pantheon as we know it was constructed during the reign of Emperor Hadrian, around 113-125 AD, replacing an earlier temple built by Marcus Agrippa in 27 BC. The original structure was destroyed by fire, and while Hadrian's version retained Agrippa's name on its pediment—a nod to the earlier structure—what now stands is entirely the work of Hadrian and his architects. The decision to keep Agrippa's name on the facade reflects Hadrian's respect for Rome's history and traditions, but the design itself was revolutionary, showcasing a shift in architectural ideals and construction techniques.

Upon approaching the Pantheon, the first feature to catch the eye is its imposing portico, supported by sixteen Corinthian columns made of Egyptian granite. Each column soars over 39 feet high, a feat of logistics and craftsmanship given their origin in distant quarries along the Nile. The triangular pediment, which once bore bronze decorations, now sits austerely atop the columns, its simplicity contrasting with the grandeur of the structure as a whole. The portico serves as a transitional space between the outside world and the awe-inspiring interior, preparing visitors for the grandeur within.

Passing through the enormous bronze doors—still original to the building—you step into the rotunda, a space that defies expectations and seems to dissolve the boundary between earth and sky. The circular floor plan, 142 feet in diameter, mirrors the height of the dome, creating a perfect sphere—a design meant to symbolize the heavens. The dome itself is a technical and artistic triumph, constructed using a combination of Roman concrete and lightweight volcanic stone called pumice. Its coffered panels, which decrease in size as they rise toward the oculus, not only reduce the weight of the structure but also add a striking visual rhythm.

The oculus, a circular opening at the dome's apex, is the only source of natural light in the Pantheon. Measuring 27 feet in diameter, this unglazed aperture serves both practical and symbolic functions. Architecturally, it reduces the weight at the dome's weakest point, while symbolically, it represents the connection between the heavens and the earthly realm below. Sunlight streams through the oculus, moving across the interior throughout the day and creating an ever-changing interplay of light and shadow. On rainy days, water enters through the oculus but is efficiently drained away by the slightly sloped marble floor and an intricate drainage system, a testament to the Romans' advanced engineering.

The interior decoration of the Pantheon further enhances its sense of harmony and grandeur. The floor, made of colorful marble slabs arranged in geometric patterns, reflects the richness of materials brought from across the Roman Empire. The walls are adorned with niches that once held statues of Roman gods, though many of these have been lost or replaced over time. The interplay between the circular and rectangular elements—seen in the niches, columns, and coffered dome—creates a sense of balance and unity, making the space feel both monumental and intimate.

The Pantheon's transformation from a pagan temple to a Christian church in 609 AD ensured its survival through centuries of political and religious upheaval. Pope Boniface IV consecrated the building as the Church of St. Mary and the Martyrs, commonly known as Santa Maria ad Martyres. This act of Christianization preserved the Pantheon from neglect or destruction, as many pagan structures were repurposed or dismantled during the Middle Ages. Over time, the church became a site of pilgrimage and devotion, while its architectural splendor continued to inspire artists and architects.

The Renaissance marked a renewed interest in the Pantheon as a source of artistic and architectural inspiration. Michelangelo famously declared it the work of angels, not men, and its influence is evident in his design of the dome of St. Peter's Basilica. The Pantheon also became the final resting place for several prominent figures, including the painter Raphael and two Italian kings, Victor Emmanuel II and Umberto I. Their tombs, marked by simple yet dignified inscriptions, add another layer of historical significance to the site.

Visiting the Pantheon today offers a unique opportunity to experience ancient architecture in its original context. Unlike many ruins, which require imagination to reconstruct their former glory, the Pantheon remains largely intact, allowing visitors to fully appreciate its scale, craftsmanship, and ingenuity. Its location in the lively Piazza della Rotonda adds to its charm, as the surrounding cafes and fountains create a vibrant atmosphere that contrasts with the solemnity of the interior.

When planning a visit, it's important to consider the Pantheon's popularity as one of Rome's most iconic landmarks. Arriving early in the morning or later in the afternoon can help you avoid the largest crowds, allowing for a more contemplative experience. Admission is free, though certain services, such as guided tours or audio guides, are available for a fee and can provide valuable insights into the building's history and significance. Photography is permitted, making it an ideal spot to capture both the grandeur of the structure and the details that make it unique.

The Pantheon's legacy extends far beyond Rome, influencing architecture around the world. From the domed churches of Renaissance Italy to the neoclassical capitols of the United States, its design principles have been adapted and reinterpreted across centuries and continents. Its enduring appeal lies not only in its technical achievements but also in its ability to evoke a sense of wonder and connection to the past. The Pantheon is more than just a building; it is a symbol of humanity's capacity for innovation, beauty, and the pursuit of the divine.

Over the centuries, the Pantheon has weathered earthquakes, invasions, and the passage of time, yet it remains as awe-inspiring as ever. Its survival is a testament to the ingenuity of its creators and the care of those who have preserved it. Standing beneath its dome, you can feel the weight of history and the brilliance of the minds that conceived it, a reminder of the heights that human civilization can achieve. The Pantheon continues to captivate and inspire, offering a timeless connection to the splendor of ancient Rome.

Trevi Fountain: Tossing Coins and Its Legends

The Trevi Fountain, or Fontana di Trevi, is one of the most iconic symbols of Rome, an enduring masterpiece of Baroque art and a magnet for millions of visitors every year. Its cascading waters, intricate sculptures, and grandiose design have made it more than just a fountain; it is a cultural and historical landmark steeped in tradition, legend, and artistry. Nestled within a small piazza in the heart of the city, the Trevi Fountain invites admirers to pause, marvel, and partake in the age-old ritual of tossing coins into its shimmering water. Yet, beyond its beauty and charm lies a story of architectural ambition, mythological inspiration, and the enduring allure of Roman culture.

The origins of the Trevi Fountain can be traced back to ancient Rome, where aqueducts were vital to the city's survival and expansion. The fountain marks the terminus of the Aqua Virgo, an aqueduct constructed in 19 BCE under the rule of Emperor Augustus. According to legend, the aqueduct was named after a young virgin who guided Roman engineers to a spring of pure water, a tale immortalized in the fountain's design. Although the original fountain was much simpler, its location at the junction of three streets—tre vie—gave the fountain its name, symbolizing the convergence of water and community.

The Trevi Fountain as it stands today was completed in 1762, the culmination of a project that spanned more than a century. Commissioned by Pope Clement XII in 1732, the fountain was designed by Nicola Salvi, who won a highly competitive contest against several renowned architects. Salvi's vision for the fountain was grand and theatrical, combining elements of classical mythology with the dramatic flair of Baroque art. Tragically, Salvi did not live to see his masterpiece completed, and the work was finished under the supervision of Giuseppe Pannini. The result is a breathtaking composition that seamlessly blends architecture, sculpture, and the natural flow of water.

Approaching the Trevi Fountain, the first thing that strikes you is its sheer scale and opulence. Standing 26 meters high and 49 meters wide, it dominates the tiny square, making it impossible to ignore. The fountain is set against the backdrop of the Palazzo Poli, whose facade was integrated into the design to enhance its grandeur. At its center is a towering figure of Oceanus, the god of the sea, standing in a chariot shaped like a shell and pulled by two sea horses. Each horse is guided by a Triton—one calm and obedient, the other wild and unruly—symbolizing the dual nature of the sea. Surrounding Oceanus are niches containing allegorical figures representing Abundance and Health, their flowing robes and serene expressions adding to the fountain's sense of majesty.

The water, a central element of the design, pours over rocky formations and into a large basin below, creating a soothing cacophony that fills the square. The sound of the water, combined with the intricate details of the sculptures and the shimmering light reflected off the surface, creates an almost hypnotic effect. It is easy to see why the Trevi Fountain has become such a beloved landmark, inspiring artists, writers, and filmmakers for centuries.

One of the most enduring traditions associated with the fountain is the ritual of tossing coins into its waters. This practice, made famous by the 1954 film *Three Coins in the Fountain*, has its roots in a much older custom. Legend has it that tossing a coin over your left shoulder with your right hand ensures that you will return to Rome someday. A second coin is said to bring romance, while a third promises marriage. The exact origins of this ritual are unclear, but it has become an integral part of the Trevi Fountain experience, with visitors from around the world participating in the hope of securing their wishes.

The coins tossed into the fountain are not merely symbolic; they also serve a practical purpose. Every night, the fountain is cleaned, and the coins are collected and donated to charity. It is estimated that over a million euros are collected annually, with the funds going to organizations that provide assistance to Rome's vulnerable populations. This practice adds a layer of social significance to the ritual, transforming a simple gesture into an act of generosity and community support.

The legends surrounding the Trevi Fountain extend beyond the coin-tossing ritual. One popular story involves the "Trevi Fountain Lovers," a pair of young people who fell in love while visiting the fountain. According to the tale, the couple pledged their devotion by drinking water from the fountain together, a tradition that has inspired countless romantic gestures over the years. Another legend speaks of the fountain's water as having magical properties, capable of granting wishes or ensuring good fortune. While these myths may lack historical grounding, they have contributed to the fountain's mystique and its status as a place of wonder and possibility.

The Trevi Fountain's cultural significance is further cemented by its appearance in numerous films and works of art. Perhaps the most famous cinematic moment is found in Federico Fellini's *La Dolce Vita* (1960), in which Anita Ekberg wades into the fountain, beckoning Marcello Mastroianni to join her. This iconic scene captures the fountain's romantic and dreamlike qualities, solidifying its place in the collective imagination. Other films, such as *Roman Holiday* and *The Lizzie McGuire Movie*, have also featured the fountain, introducing it to new generations of admirers.

Despite its enduring beauty, the Trevi Fountain has faced challenges over the centuries, including pollution, structural damage, and the impact of tourism. In recent years, restoration efforts have been undertaken to preserve the fountain for future generations. The most significant of these was completed in 2015, funded by the Italian fashion house Fendi, which contributed over two million euros to the project. The restoration involved cleaning the sculptures, repairing cracks, and installing a state-of-the-art recirculation system to improve the water's clarity. These efforts have ensured that the Trevi Fountain remains as dazzling today as it was when it was first unveiled.

Visiting the Trevi Fountain is an experience that requires patience and preparation, as it is one of Rome's most popular attractions and can be crowded at nearly any time of day. Early mornings or late evenings offer a quieter, more intimate experience, allowing you to fully appreciate the fountain's beauty without the throngs of tourists. The square itself is surrounded by cafes and gelaterias, making it an ideal spot to linger and soak in the atmosphere.

The Trevi Fountain is more than just a work of art; it is a living symbol of Rome's history, culture, and enduring appeal. Its legends and traditions have made it a place where memories are created and shared, where the past and present converge in a celebration of beauty and imagination. Tossing a coin into its waters is not just a wish for the future; it is a connection to a timeless ritual that has captivated hearts for generations. As the coins glimmer beneath the surface and the water flows endlessly, the Trevi Fountain continues to enchant, reminding us of the magic and mystery that make Rome an eternal city.

Piazza Navona: Rome's Open-Air Gallery

Piazza Navona, one of Rome's most vibrant and celebrated public squares, is a masterpiece of urban design that seamlessly blends history, art, and daily life. Its elongated, oval shape hints at its origins as the Stadium of Domitian, an ancient Roman arena built in the 1st century AD for athletic contests and public spectacles. Over centuries, the site transformed, evolving into the elegant, bustling piazza that we see today—a space where Baroque art and architecture take center stage, yet life unfolds with an unpretentious rhythm. As you wander through Piazza Navona, you are not merely visiting a historical landmark; you are stepping into a living canvas, an open-air gallery where the past and present coexist in perfect harmony.

The history of Piazza Navona is deeply rooted in ancient Rome. Built by Emperor Domitian, the stadium was designed to host agones, or athletic games, and could accommodate up to 30,000 spectators. Its long, curved shape mirrors that of a racetrack, with one end rounded and the other nearly squared. Though the stadium fell into disuse after the fall of the Roman Empire, its distinctive footprint remained, shaping the piazza that would later rise in its place. During the medieval period, the area became a marketplace, a tradition that continued well into the Renaissance. By the 17th century, the transformation of the square into a Baroque masterpiece began under the patronage of the powerful Pamphilj family, cementing its status as one of Rome's great public spaces.

At the heart of Piazza Navona lies the Fontana dei Quattro Fiumi, or Fountain of the Four Rivers, an extraordinary work by Gian Lorenzo Bernini. Commissioned in 1651 by Pope Innocent X, a member of the Pamphilj family, the fountain represents four great rivers from different continents—the Nile, the Ganges, the Danube, and the Río de la Plata—symbolizing the Church's universal reach. Each river is personified as a reclining figure, surrounded by animals and plants native to its region. The fountain's central obelisk, originally from ancient Egypt, towers above the composition, adding a sense of vertical grandeur. Bernini's genius lies in his ability to convey movement and drama; the figures seem to writhe and twist, their expressions caught in moments of tension and awe. The entire structure is alive with energy, a celebration of nature, power, and divine providence.

Directly facing the Fontana dei Quattro Fiumi is the Church of Sant'Agnese in Agone, a stunning example of Baroque architecture designed by Francesco Borromini. Dedicated to Saint Agnes, a young Christian martyr who, according to tradition, was executed in Domitian's stadium, the church stands as a testament to faith and artistic ambition. Its concave facade, flanked by twin bell towers, creates a dynamic interplay of light and shadow, drawing the eye toward the central dome. Inside, the church is a marvel of craftsmanship, with intricate stuccoes, gilded details, and frescoes that transport visitors into a celestial realm. Borromini's rivalry with Bernini is the stuff of legend, and many believe that the dramatic gestures of Bernini's river gods in the Fontana dei Quattro Fiumi are pointedly directed at Borromini's church, though this remains a matter of speculation.

Two other fountains anchor Piazza Navona, adding to its artistic richness and symmetry. At the southern end stands the Fontana del Moro, originally designed by Giacomo della Porta in the late 16th century and later enhanced by Bernini. The fountain features a central figure of a Moor wrestling a dolphin, surrounded by tritons and sea creatures that exude a sense of playful energy. At the northern end is the Fontana del Nettuno, also by Giacomo della Porta, though its central figure of Neptune battling a sea monster was added in the 19th century. Together, these fountains create a visual rhythm that guides visitors through the piazza, inviting them to pause and admire the artistry at every turn.

The piazza's vibrant atmosphere is as much a part of its charm as its architectural and artistic treasures. Street performers, musicians, and artists gather here daily, filling the square with sounds, colors, and energy. Painters set up their easels, capturing the beauty of the fountains or the lively crowds, while caricature artists offer quick sketches to amused tourists. Cafés line the perimeter of the piazza, their outdoor tables providing the perfect spot to sip an espresso or enjoy a plate of pasta while soaking in the scene. The hum of conversation, the clinking of glasses, and the occasional burst of applause for a street performer create a soundtrack that is uniquely Roman.

Throughout its history, Piazza Navona has been a stage for both grand events and everyday life. During the Baroque period, the piazza was often flooded in the summer months to create a shallow lake where mock naval battles and other spectacles could be held. Known as "La Navicella," or "The Little Ship," this practice delighted both the local population and visiting dignitaries. Though the tradition ended in the 19th century, it remains a fascinating chapter in the square's storied past. Today, the piazza hosts seasonal markets, including a famous Christmas market where stalls overflow with ornaments, sweets, and handmade crafts, adding a festive touch to this already enchanting space.

Exploring Piazza Navona also offers the chance to delve into the stories of its surrounding buildings. The Palazzo Pamphilj, now home to the Brazilian Embassy, was once the lavish residence of the Pamphilj family. Its grand halls and frescoed ceilings speak to the family's wealth and influence during the 17th century. Adjacent to the church of Sant'Agnese in Agone is the Palazzo Braschi, which houses the Museo di Roma. This museum offers a fascinating journey through the history of the city, with exhibits that include paintings, photographs, and artifacts from various periods. Each building around the piazza adds a layer of history and character, enriching the experience of visiting this remarkable place.

Piazza Navona is not without its quirks and mysteries. One of the most intriguing features is the so-called "Talking Statue" of Pasquino, located just outside the piazza. This weathered fragment of an ancient statue became a vehicle for anonymous public commentary in the form of satirical poems and notes, often criticizing political or religious figures. Known as "pasquinades," these messages were posted on the statue and read by passersby, making it an early form of public dissent. Though Pasquino is not located directly within Piazza Navona, its proximity and historical connection add an element of intrigue to the area.

Visiting Piazza Navona is an experience that rewards both curiosity and leisure. Whether you are drawn to its artistic treasures, its lively atmosphere, or its historical significance, the piazza offers something for everyone. Arriving early in the morning allows you to appreciate its beauty in relative solitude, while an evening visit reveals the square illuminated by soft lights, its fountains shimmering under the night sky. The surrounding streets, filled with boutique shops and artisanal gelaterias, invite further exploration, making Piazza Navona an ideal starting point for discovering the heart of Rome.

What makes Piazza Navona truly special is its ability to connect people across time and space. It is a place where ancient history, Renaissance art, and contemporary life converge, creating a dynamic and ever-changing tableau. Whether you are admiring Bernini's sculptures, sipping a cappuccino at a café, or simply soaking in the atmosphere, you become a part of the piazza's ongoing story. It is a reminder that Rome is not just a city of monuments and museums but a living, breathing entity where the past and present coexist in harmony.

Castel Sant'Angelo: Fortress, Museum, and History Combined

Castel Sant'Angelo, an imposing cylindrical structure on the banks of the Tiber River, is a fascinating blend of ancient Roman ingenuity, medieval fortification, Renaissance opulence, and modern-day preservation. Its history spans nearly two thousand years, making it one of Rome's most versatile and enduring landmarks. Originally conceived as a mausoleum for Emperor Hadrian, it evolved over centuries into a fortress, a papal residence, a prison, and now a museum. This layered past is etched into the very stones of the structure, making Castel Sant'Angelo a treasure trove of history and an unmissable stop for anyone seeking to understand the complexities of Rome's past.

Commissioned by Emperor Hadrian around 123 AD, Castel Sant'Angelo began as the Mausoleum of Hadrian, a monumental tomb intended to house the emperor and his family. Inspired by the grandeur of Augustus's mausoleum, Hadrian envisioned a structure that would serve as an eternal testament to his legacy. The mausoleum was constructed with a massive cylindrical core, encased in travertine marble, and crowned with a statue of Hadrian riding a chariot. The approach to the mausoleum was marked by a grand bridge, the Pons Aelius, which still stands today as the Ponte Sant'Angelo. Adorned with statues of angels, the bridge creates a stunning visual connection between the mausoleum and the rest of the city, symbolizing a passage from the earthly realm to the heavens.

Hadrian's mausoleum served its funerary purpose for several decades, housing the remains of subsequent emperors, but the decline of the Roman Empire brought significant changes. By the 5th century, Rome faced repeated invasions, and the mausoleum's strategic location near the Tiber River made it an ideal defensive stronghold. Its transformation from a tomb to a fortress began as early as 401 AD, when it was incorporated into the city's Aurelian Walls. The structure was stripped of much of its decorative marble and bronze to fortify its defenses, and its interior was repurposed with military installations. This shift in function marked the beginning of Castel Sant'Angelo's long and varied history as a fortress.

The name "Castel Sant'Angelo" originates from a pivotal event in 590 AD, during a devastating plague that swept through Rome. According to legend, Pope Gregory I had a vision of the Archangel Michael sheathing his sword atop the mausoleum, signaling the end of the epidemic. In gratitude, the pope dedicated the structure to the archangel, and a statue of Michael was later placed on its summit. This story imbued the fortress with a spiritual significance that complemented its military role, turning it into a symbol of divine protection for the city.

During the medieval period, Castel Sant'Angelo became a key defensive stronghold for the Papal States. Its location near Vatican City made it an ideal refuge for popes during times of political unrest or military threat. The fortress was connected to St. Peter's Basilica by the Passetto di Borgo, a secret passageway that allowed popes to escape from the Vatican in times of danger. This passage was famously used by Pope Clement VII during the Sack of Rome in 1527, when imperial troops besieged the city. The fortress's thick walls and strategic position ensured its survival through countless conflicts, cementing its reputation as an impregnable bastion.

The Renaissance brought significant changes to Castel Sant'Angelo, as successive popes sought to transform it into a residence worthy of their status. Lavish apartments were added, adorned with frescoes, tapestries, and ornate furniture that reflected the artistic tastes of the time. The papal apartments, still accessible to visitors today, showcase the work of prominent artists, including Perin del Vaga, a pupil of Raphael. These rooms provide a glimpse into the opulence of the Renaissance papacy, contrasting sharply with the fortress's austere exterior. The blend of military and residential features is one of the most striking aspects of Castel Sant'Angelo, highlighting its dual role as both a palace and a stronghold.

In addition to serving as a residence, Castel Sant'Angelo also functioned as a prison during the Renaissance and beyond. Its dungeons held a variety of inmates, from political prisoners to common criminals. One of the most famous prisoners was the sculptor and goldsmith Benvenuto Cellini, who was accused of embezzling from the papal treasury. Cellini's dramatic escape attempt, which involved climbing down a rope made of bed sheets, only to be recaptured, adds a layer of intrigue to the fortress's history. The prison cells, some of which can still be seen today, stand in stark contrast to the luxurious papal apartments above, underscoring the fortress's multifaceted role in Roman society.

The 19th and early 20th centuries saw Castel Sant'Angelo transition into a museum, as Italy's unification and the decline of papal power reshaped its role. Today, the Museo Nazionale di Castel Sant'Angelo houses a diverse collection of artifacts, including weaponry, paintings, sculptures, and historical documents. Each exhibit offers insight into a different period of the fortress's history, from its origins as a Roman mausoleum to its use as a military bastion and residence. The museum's layout allows visitors to explore the building's various levels, each revealing a new chapter of its story.

One of the most rewarding aspects of visiting Castel Sant'Angelo is the panoramic view from its rooftop terrace. Climbing to the top is well worth the effort, as the terrace offers breathtaking vistas of Rome, including St. Peter's Basilica, the Tiber River, and the city's sprawling rooftops. The bronze statue of the Archangel Michael, added in the 18th century, stands as a sentinel over the city, a reminder of the fortress's spiritual and historical significance. The view from the terrace provides a unique perspective on Rome, connecting the ancient, medieval, and modern aspects of the city in a single, sweeping panorama.

Practical considerations can enhance the experience of visiting Castel Sant'Angelo. Arriving early in the day is advisable, as the site can become crowded, especially during peak tourist seasons. Comfortable footwear is essential, given the fortress's many staircases and uneven surfaces. Guided tours and audio guides are available, offering valuable context that brings the building's history to life. Photography is permitted, making it an excellent opportunity to capture both the architectural details of the fortress and the stunning views from its terrace.

Castel Sant'Angelo's enduring appeal lies in its ability to embody so many facets of Rome's history. It is a place where the ambitions of emperors, the resilience of the Church, and the artistry of the Renaissance converge, creating a narrative that is as complex as it is compelling. Each layer of the structure tells a story, from the tomb of Hadrian to the papal apartments and the prison cells, making it a microcosm of the city itself. Visitors to Castel Sant'Angelo are not just exploring a building; they are immersing themselves in the ebb and flow of Rome's history, experiencing firsthand the resilience and creativity that have defined the city for millennia.

What makes Castel Sant'Angelo truly special is its ability to adapt and endure. While many ancient structures have crumbled or become relics of the past, Castel Sant'Angelo has evolved with the times, serving a variety of roles without losing its essence. It is a reminder of Rome's capacity for reinvention, a place where history is not merely preserved but continually reinterpreted. As you wander through its halls and climb its ramparts, you become part of that ongoing story, connected to the generations who have passed through its gates and left their mark on its walls.

CHAPTER 3: HIDDEN GEMS AND OFF-THE-BEATEN-PATH ADVENTURES

The Aventine Keyhole: A Secret View of St. Peter's Dome

Tucked away on the Aventine Hill, one of Rome's famed seven hills, lies a small yet intriguing mystery that has captivated both locals and travelers for generations. The Aventine Keyhole, an unassuming peephole set into the green-painted gate of the Priory of the Knights of Malta, offers one of the most enchanting and unexpected views in the Eternal City. Through this tiny aperture, perfectly framed in a corridor of manicured hedges, is an unobstructed view of the dome of St. Peter's Basilica. It is a moment of quiet wonder, a secret hidden in plain sight, and a unique way to experience the grandeur of Rome from an entirely new perspective.

The story of the Aventine Keyhole is intertwined with the history of the Aventine Hill itself, an area that has long been associated with exclusivity, reverence, and retreat. In ancient times, the Aventine was a residential area and home to temples dedicated to deities such as Diana and Minerva. Later, during the medieval and Renaissance periods, the hill became a haven for monasteries, churches, and noble families who sought its tranquility and its commanding views of the city. Today, the Aventine remains one of Rome's most serene and picturesque neighborhoods, its quiet streets lined with orange trees, elegant villas, and historic landmarks.

The keyhole itself is part of the gate to the Villa del Priorato di Malta, the headquarters of the Sovereign Military Order of Malta, a chivalric order with a history dating back to the Crusades. The villa and its gardens are private property, closed to the public, which only adds to the allure of the keyhole. The precise origins of the keyhole's famous view remain a mystery. Some believe it was deliberately designed to frame St. Peter's dome, while others suggest it was a fortunate coincidence discovered by chance. Regardless of its origins, the view is undeniably magical, a testament to the interplay between nature, architecture, and human curiosity.

Reaching the Aventine Keyhole is part of the experience, as the hill itself offers a wealth of sights and sensations that set the stage for the keyhole's quiet revelation. The climb to the top of the Aventine is a gentle one, and as you ascend, the noise and bustle of the city below begin to fade, replaced by the rustling of leaves and the distant toll of church bells. The hill is home to several iconic landmarks that hint at the area's layered history. Among these is the Basilica of Santa Sabina, a 5th-century church renowned for its austere beauty and its ancient wooden doors, which feature some of the earliest depictions of biblical scenes in Christian art.

Adjacent to Santa Sabina is the Giardino degli Aranci, or Orange Garden, a public park that offers sweeping views of the Tiber River, Trastevere, and beyond. The garden, with its fragrant orange trees and quiet benches, is a favorite spot for Romans and visitors alike, a place to pause and reflect before continuing the journey to the keyhole. From the garden, it is a short walk to Piazza dei Cavalieri di Malta, the small square that serves as the gateway to the keyhole.

The square itself is a work of art, designed in the 18th century by the Italian architect and engraver Giovanni Battista Piranesi. Best known for his dramatic etchings of Roman ruins, Piranesi brought his flair for the theatrical to this modest piazza, incorporating symbolic elements that reflect the history and mission of the Knights of Malta. The square's geometric patterns, decorative obelisks, and coats of arms create an atmosphere of quiet grandeur, setting the stage for the keyhole's understated charm.

Approaching the green gate, you might not immediately notice the tiny aperture that has drawn so much attention. The keyhole is unmarked and unassuming, blending seamlessly into its surroundings. Yet, as you lean in and peer through, the scene that unfolds is nothing short of breathtaking. The perfectly centered dome of St. Peter's Basilica rises in the distance, framed by the dark green hedges of the garden on the other side of the gate. The effect is one of surreal clarity and depth, as if you are looking through a portal to another world. The alignment is so precise that it feels deliberate, a secret gift left by an anonymous hand.

What makes the Aventine Keyhole so special is not just the view itself but the sense of discovery and intimacy it provides. Unlike Rome's grand monuments and bustling piazzas, the keyhole offers a moment of quiet wonder, a chance to connect with the city on a more personal level. There is no ticket booth, no guided tour, no crowds jockeying for position. It is simply you and the view, a private dialogue between the past and the present, the seen and the unseen. For a brief moment, you are part of a centuries-old tradition of curiosity and delight, sharing in a secret that transcends time and place.

The keyhole has inspired countless reactions, from smiles of surprise to contemplative silence. For some, it serves as a metaphor for perspective, a reminder that even the smallest openings can reveal great beauty. For others, it is a symbol of Rome itself, a city that rewards those who take the time to look deeper, to explore beyond the obvious. The keyhole's charm lies in its simplicity, its ability to transform an ordinary gate into a window to the extraordinary.

Visiting the Aventine Keyhole is best done early in the morning or late in the evening, when the light is soft and the hill is at its most tranquil. The experience is even more magical at night, when the dome of St. Peter's is softly illuminated, glowing like a jewel against the dark sky. While there is no cost to view the keyhole, it is important to respect the privacy of the Priory of the Knights of Malta and the people who live and work in the area. Quiet appreciation is the unspoken rule here, a way to honor the serenity of the space and the spirit of discovery it embodies.

The Aventine Keyhole is not a grand monument or a famous museum, yet it captures the essence of what makes Rome so captivating. It is a city of layers, of secrets waiting to be uncovered, of moments that surprise and delight when you least expect them. The keyhole is a reminder that beauty often lies in the details, in the small and the overlooked, and that sometimes the most memorable experiences are the ones you stumble upon by chance. As you step back from the gate and begin your descent from the Aventine Hill, the view through the keyhole lingers in your mind, a lasting image of Rome's endless capacity to enchant and inspire.

Trastevere: Rome's Bohemian Neighborhood

Trastevere, a name that translates to "beyond the Tiber," is a neighborhood that captures the soul of Rome like no other. Nestled on the west bank of the Tiber River, this historic quarter has long been a haven for artists, rebels, and dreamers. Its narrow, cobblestone streets wind through a labyrinth of ochre-colored buildings adorned with ivy and laundry lines, creating an atmosphere that feels both timeless and alive. Trastevere is a place where the past whispers through ancient churches and medieval alleys, yet the present pulsates with the energy of vibrant piazzas, eclectic cafes, and a thriving nightlife. It is a neighborhood that defies easy categorization, blending bohemian charm with deep historical roots.

The story of Trastevere begins in antiquity when the area was home to the Etruscans before being absorbed into the Roman

Republic. In those early days, it was considered a working-class district, housing fishermen, sailors, and immigrants, including a significant Jewish population. Its location outside the city's original boundaries gave it a unique identity, one that was both connected to and distinct from the heart of Rome. Over time, Trastevere became a melting pot of cultures, a characteristic that remains evident in its diverse architecture and culinary traditions.

Walking through Trastevere feels like stepping into a living museum. The streets are lined with buildings that tell stories of centuries gone by, from medieval towers and Renaissance palaces to humble, weathered facades that exude character. The neighborhood's layout, with its irregular streets and hidden corners, reflects its organic growth over millennia, a stark contrast to the orderly grids of Rome's more modern districts. This maze-like quality invites exploration, encouraging visitors to lose themselves in its charm and stumble upon unexpected treasures.

One of Trastevere's most striking features is its collection of churches, each with its own unique history and artistic significance. The Basilica of Santa Maria in Trastevere is the neighborhood's crown jewel, a masterpiece of early Christian art and architecture. Believed to be one of the oldest churches in Rome, it is said to mark the spot where oil miraculously flowed from the earth at the time of Christ's birth. The basilica's golden mosaics, created by Pietro Cavallini in the 13th century, glitter with depictions of the Virgin Mary and saints, their intricate details a testament to the skill of medieval artisans. Stepping into the church, you are enveloped by a sense of sacred tranquility, a moment of quiet reflection amidst the bustle of the city.

Just a short walk away is the Church of Santa Cecilia in Trastevere, dedicated to the patron saint of music. The church's unassuming exterior belies the treasures within, including a stunning Baroque sculpture of St. Cecilia by

Stefano Maderno and an ancient crypt adorned with frescoes. Legend has it that St. Cecilia sang to God even as she faced martyrdom, a story that resonates in the church's ethereal atmosphere. Visiting these sacred spaces offers a glimpse into Trastevere's spiritual heritage, one that is deeply woven into the fabric of the neighborhood.

Trastevere is not just a place of worship and history; it is also a hub of cultural and social life. Its piazzas serve as communal living rooms where locals and visitors gather to eat, drink, and celebrate. Piazza Santa Maria in Trastevere, with its iconic fountain and lively atmosphere, is the heart of the neighborhood. By day, it is a place to enjoy a coffee or gelato while watching street performers and artists at work. By night, it transforms into a vibrant social scene, with laughter and music spilling out from the surrounding bars and restaurants.

One of Trastevere's defining characteristics is its culinary scene, which combines traditional Roman fare with innovative twists. The neighborhood's trattorias and osterias serve up classics like cacio e pepe, carbonara, and saltimbocca, dishes that embody the simplicity and richness of Roman cuisine. For those seeking something more contemporary, Trastevere offers an array of modern eateries and fusion restaurants that reflect the area's creative spirit. Whether you're dining at a centuries-old trattoria or a trendy bistro, the food in Trastevere is a celebration of flavor and authenticity.

The neighborhood's bohemian reputation is further cemented by its vibrant arts scene. Trastevere has long been a magnet for writers, painters, and musicians drawn to its inspiring atmosphere and sense of community. Its streets are dotted with galleries, artisan workshops, and independent bookstores, each offering a glimpse into the neighborhood's creative soul. The Janiculum Hill, which rises above Trastevere, provides a stunning backdrop for this artistic enclave. From its panoramic terrace, you can take in sweeping views of Rome, a vista that has inspired countless works of art and literature.

Trastevere's nightlife is as diverse as its history, catering to a wide range of tastes and moods. The neighborhood comes alive after dark, its narrow streets illuminated by the warm glow of lanterns and the hum of conversation. Traditional wine bars and enotecas offer a cozy setting for sampling local vintages, while lively pubs and cocktail bars attract a younger crowd. Live music venues and open-air performances add to the festive atmosphere, making Trastevere a destination for night owls and culture enthusiasts alike. The neighborhood's nightlife is not about flashy clubs or high-end lounges; it is about connection, conversation, and the simple pleasure of enjoying good company in a beautiful setting.

Despite its popularity, Trastevere has managed to retain its authentic charm, a quality that sets it apart from more tourist-heavy areas of Rome. Its residents, known as Trasteverini, are fiercely proud of their neighborhood and its traditions. This pride is evident in the annual Festa de' Noantri, a summer festival that celebrates the Virgin Mary with processions, music, and street fairs. The festival is a reminder of Trastevere's strong sense of community and its ability to balance its historical roots with its contemporary vibrancy.

Exploring Trastevere requires no set itinerary; its magic lies in the act of wandering. Take the time to meander through its streets, pausing to admire a hidden courtyard, a weathered fresco, or a vine-covered wall. Visit its markets, where vendors sell everything from fresh produce to handmade crafts. Stop for a coffee at a sun-dappled cafe or linger over a glass of wine at a rustic enoteca. Each moment spent in Trastevere is an opportunity to connect with the neighborhood's unique spirit, to experience a side of Rome that feels both timeless and refreshingly real.

Trastevere's allure is difficult to define, yet impossible to deny. It is a place where contradictions coexist in harmony: ancient and modern, sacred and profane, lively and serene. It is a neighborhood that invites you to slow down, to savor the details, and to lose yourself in its charm. Whether you are drawn to its history, its art, its food, or simply its atmosphere, Trastevere offers an experience that lingers long after you leave. It is not just a part of Rome; it is a state of mind, a reminder that beauty and inspiration can be found in the most unexpected places.

Testaccio Market: A Foodie's Paradise

Tucked away in the historic Roman neighborhood of Testaccio, the Testaccio Market is an unmissable destination for anyone who wants to experience the authentic flavors of Rome. More than just a marketplace, it is a vibrant gathering point where food, culture, and community intersect. Built on centuries of tradition yet infused with a modern edge, the Testaccio Market offers an unparalleled culinary journey through the heart of Roman gastronomy. From fresh produce and artisanal goods to street food and innovative cuisine, it reveals the soul of this working-class district turned foodie paradise.

Testaccio itself is steeped in history, its identity rooted in its role as Rome's ancient center for trade and commerce. The neighborhood takes its name from Monte Testaccio, an artificial hill made entirely of discarded amphorae—terra-cotta jars that once carried olive oil and wine from across the Mediterranean. These shards, carefully stacked over centuries, are a testament to Testaccio's importance as a trade hub during the height of the Roman Empire. Even today, the district retains a raw, unpolished charm that sets it apart from the tourist-heavy parts of the city. It is a place where tradition meets innovation, and nowhere is this more evident than in the Testaccio Market.

The market, known locally as Mercato di Testaccio, has a history that mirrors the evolution of the neighborhood itself. Originally an outdoor market held in Piazza Testaccio, it moved to its current location on Via Galvani in 2012. The move was controversial at the time, as locals feared that a modern structure might strip the market of its historic character. However, the transition was executed with care, resulting in a sleek, contemporary space that retains the lively, community-focused spirit of the traditional market. The new location offers a clean, well-organized environment, more accessible facilities, and a mix of old and new vendors that cater to both longtime residents and curious visitors.

Stepping into the market is an assault on the senses in the best possible way. The air is filled with the mingling aromas of fresh herbs, ripe fruit, roasting meats, and simmering sauces. Stalls are brimming with vibrant displays of seasonal produce, colorful spices, and freshly baked bread. Vendors call out to passersby, their voices adding to the symphony of sounds that defines the space. It is a place where the energy is palpable, where every corner offers a new discovery and every interaction feels personal.

The produce section is a highlight of the market, offering a dazzling array of fruits and vegetables that reflect Italy's agricultural bounty. Juicy blood oranges, sun-ripened tomatoes, and fragrant basil are just a few of the staples you'll find here, all sourced from local farms. The vendors, many of whom have been selling at the market for generations, are a wealth of knowledge. They are quick to offer tips on how to select the best ingredients or share recipes for traditional Roman dishes. This connection between producer and consumer is a cornerstone of the Testaccio Market experience, fostering a sense of trust and community that is increasingly rare in today's world.

Beyond the produce, the market is a treasure trove of specialty items that cater to food lovers of all kinds. Cheese enthusiasts will delight in the selection of pecorino, ricotta, and aged Parmigiano-Reggiano, while carnivores can explore stalls offering everything from freshly butchered cuts to cured meats like guanciale and prosciutto. Seafood lovers will find an impressive variety of fish and shellfish, often displayed on beds of crushed ice for maximum freshness. These ingredients form the foundation of Roman cuisine, and the market provides an opportunity to see them in their raw, unadulterated form, ready to be transformed into culinary masterpieces.

The prepared food section of the market is where Testaccio truly shines, offering a mix of traditional Roman street food and innovative dishes that push the boundaries of Italian cuisine. A visit to Mordi e Vai, one of the market's most famous stalls, is practically mandatory. Run by Sergio Esposito, a butcher turned sandwich maestro, Mordi e Vai serves panini stuffed with classic Roman fillings like braised beef, tripe, and oxtail. Each bite is a burst of flavor, a testament to the simplicity and richness of Roman cooking. Nearby, you might find stalls offering suppli—fried rice balls filled with cheese and ragù—or pizza al taglio, rectangular slices of pizza sold by weight and topped with everything from zucchini flowers to spicy salami.

For the more adventurous eater, the market also offers a chance to sample Rome's quinto quarto cuisine, a tradition rooted in Testaccio's history as the city's butchery district. Quinto quarto, or "fifth quarter," refers to the offal and less commonly used parts of the animal, such as liver, heart, and intestines. These ingredients, once considered humble fare, have been elevated into delicacies through the creativity of Roman cooks. Dishes like trippa alla romana (tripe in tomato sauce) and coda alla vaccinara (oxtail stew) are celebrated for their bold flavors and rich textures. At the market, you can see these ingredients up close and even taste them freshly prepared, gaining a deeper appreciation for this unique aspect of Roman culinary heritage.

One of the most striking aspects of the Testaccio Market is its ability to balance tradition with modernity. Alongside stalls that have been in operation for decades, you'll find newcomers offering contemporary takes on Italian cuisine. Vegan and vegetarian options, once rare in a city known for its love of meat and cheese, are becoming increasingly common. Artisanal products, such as craft beer, organic olive oil, and gourmet chocolate, cater to modern tastes while still respecting the market's emphasis on quality and authenticity. This fusion of old and new makes the market a dynamic space that evolves with the times while staying true to its roots.

The market is not just a place to shop or eat; it is a hub of social interaction and community life. Locals gather here not only to buy groceries but also to catch up with friends, exchange gossip, and share a coffee at one of the market's cafes. For visitors, it is an opportunity to witness the rhythms of daily life in Testaccio, to see how food is not just sustenance but a way of connecting with others. The market's layout, with its open stalls and communal seating areas, encourages conversation and interaction, breaking down barriers between strangers and creating a sense of belonging.

Beyond the food, the Testaccio Market also offers a glimpse into the neighborhood's creative spirit. Some stalls sell handmade crafts, vintage clothing, and unique souvenirs, providing an alternative to the mass-produced items found in tourist shops. These treasures, often made by local artisans, reflect the individuality and creativity that define Testaccio as a whole. Whether you're picking up a jar of artisanal honey or a hand-painted ceramic plate, you're taking home a piece of the neighborhood's soul.

A visit to the Testaccio Market is best savored slowly, with plenty of time to wander, taste, and explore. Arriving early in the morning ensures the freshest produce and the chance to see the market at its liveliest, as vendors set up their stalls and locals begin their daily shopping. While Saturdays are the busiest, with a lively and festive atmosphere, weekdays offer a more relaxed experience, allowing you to interact with vendors without feeling rushed. Comfortable shoes are a must, as the market's sprawling layout invites exploration. Whether you're a seasoned foodie or simply curious about Roman culture, the Testaccio Market offers something for everyone.

Testaccio Market is more than just a place to buy food; it is a celebration of Rome's culinary heritage and its ability to adapt to the modern world without losing its essence. It is a place where history, culture, and flavor come together, creating an experience that is as enriching as it is delicious. Each visit offers a chance to learn, to connect, and to be inspired by the passion and creativity of the people who bring the market to life. As you leave, laden with ingredients, souvenirs, or simply memories, you carry with you a piece of Testaccio's heart—a reminder of the power of food to bring people together and tell a story that spans generations.

San Clemente Basilica: A Journey Through Layers of History

San Clemente Basilica is not just a church; it is an extraordinary journey through time, a place where centuries of history are stacked like the pages of a book waiting to be explored. Nestled in a quiet corner of Rome, just a short walk from the Colosseum, this basilica offers an unparalleled experience for those who seek to understand the layers of Rome's past. What sets San Clemente apart is its unique structure: three distinct levels, each representing a different era, built one on top of the other. From a 12th-century basilica, descending into a 4th-century church, and finally reaching the depths of a 1st-century Roman house and Mithraic temple, visiting San Clemente is like peeling back the layers of a living archaeological artifact.

The present-day basilica, built in the 12th century, is a stunning example of Romanesque architecture blended with Byzantine art. Upon entering the church, you are immediately struck by its harmonious proportions and the exquisite mosaics that adorn the apse. The golden mosaic of the Triumph of the Cross is a masterpiece, depicting a radiant cross surrounded by intricate vine scrolls, peacocks, and other symbolic figures. The imagery is rich with theological meaning, representing the triumph of Christ over death and the promise of eternal life. The floor of the basilica is equally mesmerizing, paved with a Cosmatesque design—a geometric mosaic style crafted by the Cosmati family, known for their skillful use of colored marble and glass. Every detail in this uppermost layer of San Clemente speaks to the craftsmanship and devotion of the medieval church.

Yet, as remarkable as the 12th-century basilica is, it is only the beginning of the journey. A small staircase leads down to the second level, revealing a 4th-century Christian church hidden beneath the medieval structure. This older basilica, constructed shortly after the legalization of Christianity under Emperor Constantine, is a stark contrast to the ornate church above. Its walls are faded, its columns worn with time, but the sense of history is palpable. Fragments of frescoes still cling to the walls, offering glimpses of early Christian art. One particularly vivid fresco depicts the legend of Saint Clement, the church's namesake and the fourth pope of the Catholic Church. According to tradition, Saint Clement was martyred by being tied to an anchor and thrown into the sea—a story that is poignantly illustrated in faded yet evocative detail.

As you wander through the 4th-century basilica, it becomes clear that this space was more than just a place of worship. It was a gathering point for the early Christian community, a sanctuary in a time when Christianity was still finding its place in a predominantly pagan world. The layout of the church, with its central nave and side aisles, reflects the architectural transition from Roman civic buildings to Christian worship spaces. This level of San Clemente is a testament to the resilience and adaptability of the early Church, a reminder of the challenges faced by those who practiced their faith in a time of uncertainty.

The journey does not end here. Another staircase descends even further, plunging visitors into the depths of ancient Rome. On this lowest level lies the remains of a 1st-century Roman house and a Mithraeum, a temple dedicated to the god Mithras. The Mithraic cult was a mystery religion popular among Roman soldiers and officials, characterized by its secretive rituals and underground temples. The Mithraeum at San Clemente is remarkably well-preserved, with an altar depicting Mithras slaying a bull—a central motif in the religion's iconography. Standing in this shadowy space, it is easy to imagine the flicker of oil lamps and the murmured prayers of worshippers who gathered here nearly two millennia ago.

The Roman house adjacent to the Mithraeum adds yet another layer to the story of San Clemente. Its walls reveal traces of frescoes, and its rooms provide a glimpse into daily life in ancient Rome. One of the most intriguing features of this level is the sound of water flowing beneath the structure. This is a remnant of a Roman aqueduct that still carries water through the area, a reminder of the engineering marvels that supported the city's growth and prosperity. The presence of the aqueduct ties the site to the broader urban fabric of ancient Rome, connecting it to the systems and infrastructure that defined the empire.

What makes San Clemente so extraordinary is not just the physical layers of history but the way they interact and inform one another. Each level builds upon the one below it, creating a continuous narrative that spans centuries. The site is a microcosm of Rome itself, a city where the old is never truly erased but rather repurposed and integrated into the new. This sense of continuity is one of the reasons why San

Clemente resonates so deeply with those who visit. It is a place where history feels alive, where the past is not a distant memory but a tangible presence.

The experience of visiting San Clemente is deeply immersive, offering more than just a visual feast. The descent through the layers of the basilica is accompanied by a change in atmosphere—the light grows dimmer, the air cooler, and the sounds of the modern world fade away. It is a sensory journey as much as an intellectual one, a chance to step out of time and into the lives of those who came before. Each level tells its own story, yet together they form a cohesive narrative that speaks to the enduring spirit of Rome.

Exploring San Clemente also provides a unique opportunity to reflect on the concept of sacred space. What began as a Roman house and pagan temple was transformed into a Christian church, and later into a medieval basilica. Each iteration of the site reflects the beliefs and values of its time, yet all are united by a sense of reverence and a desire to create a space for connection—whether with the divine, the community, or the self. This continuity of purpose is a powerful reminder of the ways in which humanity seeks meaning and transcendence, regardless of the era or the faith.

Practical considerations can enhance the experience of visiting San Clemente. The site is best explored with a guide or an audio tour, as the layers of history are complex and richly detailed. Comfortable shoes are essential, as the descent through the basilica involves navigating uneven staircases and floors. Photography is typically not permitted inside the basilica, allowing visitors to focus fully on the experience rather than capturing it through a lens. Arriving early in the day or during off-peak hours ensures a quieter visit, allowing for a more intimate connection with the space.

San Clemente is not as well-known as some of Rome's other landmarks, yet it offers an experience that is every bit as profound. It is a place that rewards curiosity and invites contemplation, a reminder that history is not a static record but a dynamic, living force. Each layer of the basilica adds depth and texture to the story of Rome, revealing the city's capacity for reinvention and its enduring connection to the past. For those who take the time to explore its depths, San Clemente offers a journey unlike any other—a descent into history that leaves you with a deeper appreciation for the layers of life that make Rome eternal.

The Catacombs of Rome: Exploring Underground Mysteries

Beneath the bustling streets of Rome lie the catacombs, a network of underground burial chambers that stretch for miles, forming a labyrinth of tunnels shrouded in mystery and history. These subterranean corridors, carved out of soft volcanic rock known as tuff, are more than just ancient cemeteries—they are silent witnesses to the evolution of faith, culture, and survival in the Eternal City. Visiting the catacombs is a step into a hidden world where the living and the dead once coexisted, a world that reveals the resilience of early Christian communities and their determination to preserve their beliefs during times of persecution. Each catacomb holds its own story, etched into the walls and painted in frescoes that have endured the passage of centuries.

The catacombs emerged during the 2nd century AD, at a time when Christianity was still a fledgling religion in the Roman Empire. While early Christians practiced their faith in secrecy, burial rituals were of paramount importance to their spiritual lives. Roman law prohibited burials within the city walls, which led to the development of cemeteries on the outskirts of the city. Unlike their pagan counterparts, who customarily cremated their dead, Christians believed in the bodily resurrection and opted for burial. This practice required large amounts of space, and the soft tuff beneath Rome provided the ideal material for excavating intricate underground cemeteries.

The earliest catacombs were simple, narrow tunnels with niches carved into the walls to hold the bodies of the deceased. Over time, as the Christian population grew, these burial sites expanded into vast underground complexes with multiple levels. The niches, known as loculi, were often sealed with slabs of marble or terracotta, inscribed with the names of the deceased and symbols of faith, such as the fish, the anchor, or the Chi-Rho. Wealthier families commissioned more elaborate tombs, called arcosolia, which featured arched recesses and were often decorated with frescoes. These artistic elements not only honored the dead but also served as visual expressions of the Christian faith in an era when literacy was limited.

Among the most famous catacombs in Rome are the Catacombs of San Sebastiano, San Callisto, and Domitilla, each offering a unique glimpse into this underground world. The Catacombs of San Sebastiano, located along the Appian Way, are believed to have housed the remains of Saints Peter and Paul at one point, making them a site of pilgrimage for early Christians. The catacombs take their name from Saint Sebastian, a martyr of the early Church whose relics are still venerated in the basilica above. The tunnels here are notable for their graffiti, left by pilgrims who etched prayers and names into the walls as acts of devotion.

The Catacombs of San Callisto, also on the Appian Way, are among the largest and most significant in Rome, covering an area of over 37 acres. These catacombs served as the official cemetery of the Roman Church in the 3rd century and are the final resting place of several popes, earning them the nickname "the cemetery of the popes." The Crypt of the Popes is a highlight of this site, where inscriptions in Greek and Latin commemorate the martyrs and leaders of the early Church. The frescoes in San Callisto are particularly striking, depicting scenes from both the Old and New Testaments, such as the Good Shepherd, Noah's Ark, and the raising of Lazarus. These images provided comfort and hope to the early Christians, reinforcing their belief in salvation and eternal life.

The Catacombs of Domitilla, named after Flavia Domitilla, a member of the imperial family who converted to Christianity, are the oldest and most extensive of Rome's catacombs. They include a subterranean basilica dedicated to Saints Nereus and Achilleus, two soldiers who were martyred for their faith. The frescoes here are among the best-preserved in Rome, offering a vivid snapshot of early Christian iconography. One notable fresco depicts a banquet scene, interpreted as a representation of the Eucharist or the heavenly feast awaiting the faithful in the afterlife. Walking through the Catacombs of Domitilla, one can sense the reverence and care with which these spaces were created, reflecting the deep spiritual convictions of those who built and used them.

The catacombs were not merely places of burial; they also served as sanctuaries for worship and community gatherings, particularly during periods of persecution. While the notion of Christians hiding in the catacombs to escape Roman authorities has been largely debunked, it is true that these underground spaces provided a safe haven for clandestine worship. Small chapels, called cubicula, were carved out of the rock and adorned with altars and frescoes, creating sacred spaces where early Christians could gather to celebrate the Eucharist and honor their martyrs. The sense of solidarity and resilience fostered in these hidden chambers played a crucial role in the survival and growth of Christianity during its formative years.

The decline of the Roman Empire and the eventual legalization of Christianity in the 4th century marked a turning point for the catacombs. With the construction of above-ground churches and cemeteries, the underground burial sites gradually fell out of use. However, they remained places of pilgrimage, revered for their connection to the martyrs and saints buried within. During the Middle Ages, many of the relics were transferred to churches in the city for safekeeping, and the catacombs were largely forgotten until their rediscovery in the 16th century by Antonio Bosio, an archaeologist often referred to as the "Columbus of the Catacombs."

Today, the catacombs are carefully preserved and managed, offering visitors a rare opportunity to explore this hidden facet of Rome's history. Walking through the dimly lit corridors, with their walls lined with ancient tombs, is a humbling experience. The air is cool and heavy with the weight of centuries, and the silence is broken only by the soft echo of footsteps. It is a place that invites reflection, not only on the lives of those who were buried here but also on the enduring power of faith and community.

Visiting the catacombs requires a sense of respect and reverence, as these are not merely historical sites but sacred spaces that continue to hold spiritual significance for many. Guided tours are essential, as the labyrinthine nature of the tunnels can be disorienting, and the expertise of the guides brings the history and symbolism of the catacombs to life. Practical considerations include wearing comfortable shoes and a light jacket, as the underground environment can be cool and uneven. Photography is generally not allowed, ensuring that the focus remains on the experience rather than capturing it through a lens.

The catacombs offer a unique perspective on Rome, one that contrasts sharply with the grandeur of its above-ground monuments. While the Colosseum, the Forum, and the Vatican speak to the power and splendor of the city, the catacombs reveal a quieter, more intimate side of its history. They are a testament to the resilience of the human spirit and the ways in which people have sought to create meaning, even in the face of adversity. For those willing to venture beneath the surface, the catacombs provide an unforgettable journey into the depths of Rome's past, a journey that resonates with the stories of those who lived, worshiped, and found solace in these underground chambers.

The Appian Way: Ancient Roads and Aqueducts

Stretching like a ribbon of stone from the heart of Rome to the southern reaches of Italy, the Appian Way—known in Latin as the Via Appia—stands as one of the most remarkable feats of engineering from the Roman Republic. This ancient road, often referred to as the "Queen of Roads," was not only a practical artery for trade and military campaigns but also a symbol of Rome's ambition and ingenuity. Constructed in 312 BC under the direction of the censor Appius Claudius Caecus, the road connected Rome to Capua, and eventually extended as far as Brindisi. To walk along the Appian Way today is to trace the footsteps of emperors, soldiers, merchants, and pilgrims who once journeyed along this path, their lives woven into the stones beneath your feet.

The Appian Way was a revolutionary project for its time, demonstrating the Romans' unparalleled expertise in infrastructure. Its construction was a meticulous process that began with excavating a trench and layering it with materials to ensure durability. Large stones formed the foundation, followed by gravel and smaller stones, all compacted together to create a flat, even surface. The final layer consisted of massive basalt slabs, precisely cut and fitted to form a stable and enduring roadway. The slight curve of the road's surface, known as cambering, allowed rainwater to drain off efficiently, preventing erosion and ensuring the road's longevity. This attention to detail made the Appian Way one of the most durable roads in history, with sections still intact more than two millennia later.

The road's primary purpose was military. During the Samnite Wars, the Appian Way enabled Roman legions to march swiftly southward, securing the Republic's control over the Italian peninsula. Its strategic importance cannot be overstated; the road allowed for the rapid deployment of troops and supplies, giving Rome a significant advantage in warfare. Over time, however, the road's utility expanded beyond military use. Merchants used it to transport goods ranging from olive oil and wine to textiles and spices, fostering economic growth and connecting distant regions of the empire. The road also became a conduit for cultural exchange, facilitating the movement of ideas, art, and people across the Roman world.

Walking the Appian Way today, one cannot help but marvel at the remnants of its grandeur. The road begins at the Porta San Sebastiano, part of the ancient Aurelian Walls, and stretches outward into the countryside. The initial stretch of the road is flanked by towering cypress trees and lined with ruins that tell the story of Rome's past. Among these are the tombs and mausoleums of prominent Roman families, who chose to be buried along the road as a display of wealth and status. The Tomb of Cecilia Metella, a massive cylindrical structure built for the daughter of a Roman consul, is one of the most striking examples. Its imposing silhouette serves as a reminder of the road's dual role as a thoroughfare and a place of memory.

Further along the Appian Way, the landscape begins to change. The bustling noise of Rome fades into the serene quiet of the countryside, where ancient aqueducts rise like skeletal giants against the horizon. These aqueducts, engineering marvels in their own right, were essential to the functioning of the Roman Empire. The Aqua Appia, Rome's first aqueduct, was constructed concurrently with the Appian Way, underscoring the Romans' commitment to infrastructure. Built to transport fresh water from distant springs to the city, aqueducts like the Aqua Appia and the Aqua Claudia were feats of both engineering and aesthetics. Their arches, constructed with precision and symmetry, remain iconic symbols of Roman ingenuity.

The aqueducts and the Appian Way were often intertwined, both physically and functionally. In some sections, the aqueducts ran parallel to the road, supplying water to travelers and the villas that dotted the landscape. These villas, belonging to wealthy Romans, were luxurious retreats that showcased the owners' affluence. Many were equipped with baths, gardens, and elaborate mosaics, all made possible by the aqueducts' reliable water supply. The synergy between the road and the aqueducts exemplifies the Romans' ability to integrate infrastructure into their daily lives seamlessly.

One of the most evocative aspects of the Appian Way is its role as a silent witness to history, both triumphant and tragic. Along its path, the road bore witness to the march of victorious armies returning to Rome, their spoils of war on display for jubilant crowds. Yet, it was also the site of one of Rome's darkest episodes: the crucifixion of 6,000 slaves following the suppression of Spartacus's revolt in 71 BC. Their bodies lined the road from Capua to Rome, a brutal display of the Republic's power and a grim reminder of the cost of rebellion. The juxtaposition of glory and suffering along the Appian Way reflects the complexities of Roman history, where progress and brutality often went hand in hand.

Exploring the Appian Way today offers a unique perspective on the layers of Rome's past. The road is not merely an artifact; it is a living corridor that continues to connect people and places. Cyclists and pedestrians share the path with archaeologists and historians, all drawn by the allure of its history. Along the way, visitors can explore sites such as the Catacombs of San Sebastiano and San Callisto, underground burial chambers that provide another dimension to the road's narrative. These catacombs, hidden beneath the surface, remind us that the Appian Way is as much about what lies below as what stretches above.

Preserving the Appian Way is an ongoing challenge, as urban development and natural erosion threaten its integrity. Efforts by organizations such as the Parco della Caffarella and the Appia Antica Regional Park aim to protect and restore this invaluable heritage. These conservation initiatives ensure that future generations can experience the road in all its historical and cultural richness. Walking tours, guided excursions, and archaeological studies all contribute to a deeper understanding of the Appian Way and its significance.

Experiencing the Appian Way requires a sense of curiosity and a willingness to slow down. Unlike Rome's more famous landmarks, the road demands patience and attention to detail. Each step reveals a new layer of history, whether it's a fragment of an inscription, a weathered milestone, or the faint outline of a chariot's groove worn into the stone. These details bring the road to life, transforming it from a static relic into a dynamic narrative of Rome's evolution.

The Appian Way is more than just a road; it is a symbol of connection, resilience, and innovation. It represents the ambition of a civilization that sought to unite its far-flung territories through infrastructure and ingenuity. It is a testament to the enduring legacy of Rome, a city that continues to inspire awe and admiration. For those who walk its ancient stones, the Appian Way offers not only a journey through time but also a deeper appreciation for the foundations upon which modern civilization is built.

Villa Doria Pamphili: Rome's Largest Public Park

Villa Doria Pamphili offers an oasis of tranquility amid the constant pace of Rome, a sprawling expanse of nature, history, and art that provides a welcome escape from the city's urban intensity. As Rome's largest public park, it covers over 180 hectares of rolling hills, lush gardens, shaded paths, and historical structures, making it a destination that appeals to locals and visitors alike. Nestled on the Janiculum Hill in the Monteverde district, the villa is far more than just a park—it is a slice of Roman history, an architectural gem, and a place where nature and culture coexist harmoniously.

The origins of Villa Doria Pamphili date back to the 17th century, when it was established as a private estate by the Pamphili family, one of Rome's most prominent noble families. In 1630, Pamphilio Pamphili—whose family would later produce Pope Innocent X—acquired the land and commissioned a villa to serve as both a residence and a symbol of the family's wealth and cultural influence. The villa became a showcase of Baroque architecture and landscaping, blending grandeur and elegance in a manner befitting the prestige of the Pamphili name. Over the centuries, the estate passed through various hands, eventually becoming public property in the 20th century. Today, it stands as a testament to the layered history of Rome, open for all to explore and enjoy.

One of the most striking features of Villa Doria Pamphili is its Casino del Bel Respiro, also known as the Villa Algardi. This Baroque villa, designed by the architect Alessandro Algardi, is an architectural masterpiece that reflects the opulence of the Pamphili family at its zenith. The building's symmetrical façade, adorned with classical motifs and intricate details, exudes a sense of refinement and balance. Inside, the villa's frescoed ceilings and ornate decorations speak to the artistic tastes of the era, although the interior is not typically open to the public. Surrounding the villa is a formal Italian garden, meticulously designed with geometric flowerbeds, hedges, and fountains that create a sense of order and harmony. The garden's symmetry and precision contrast beautifully with the wild, sprawling nature of the park beyond, offering visitors a glimpse into the dualities that define the estate.

The park itself is a vast and diverse landscape that invites exploration and discovery. Its paths meander through dense woodlands, open meadows, and gently sloping hills, providing a variety of terrains and vistas. Ancient pines, cypress trees, and oaks tower above, offering shade and a sense of seclusion, while open fields dotted with wildflowers create spaces for picnics, relaxation, or quiet contemplation. The park's size and layout make it easy to find a quiet corner to escape the crowds, whether you're looking to read a book under a tree, take a leisurely stroll, or simply listen to the rustling leaves and birdsong.

Throughout the park, remnants of its historical past reveal themselves in subtle and unexpected ways. Fountains, statues, and ornamental features are scattered across the grounds, blending seamlessly with the natural surroundings. The Fontana del Giglio, or Fountain of the Lily, is one such example, its elegant design a nod to the Baroque aesthetic that characterizes much of the estate. Nearby, you might come across an ancient aqueduct, its weathered arches standing as a reminder of Rome's engineering prowess and the estate's connection to the city's broader history.

One of the unique aspects of Villa Doria Pamphili is its ability to cater to a wide range of interests and activities. For fitness enthusiasts, the park's extensive network of trails provides ample opportunities for jogging, cycling, or even yoga in the open air. Families are drawn to the park for its expansive green spaces, where children can run freely, fly kites, or play games. Dog owners find it a haven for their pets, with designated areas where dogs can roam off-leash. For those with a passion for history and art, the park's architectural features and historical significance offer endless opportunities for exploration and appreciation. In every corner of the park, there is something to engage the senses and nourish the spirit.

The park also boasts a rich biodiversity, making it a destination for nature lovers and birdwatchers. Its varied habitats support a wide range of flora and fauna, from common species to those less frequently seen in urban environments. You might spot a fox darting through the underbrush, hear the call of a woodpecker echoing through the trees, or catch a glimpse of a kestrel soaring overhead. The park's ponds and wetlands attract herons, ducks, and other waterfowl, adding to the sense of being immersed in a living ecosystem. This connection to nature is one of the reasons why Villa Doria Pamphili is cherished by Romans as a place to recharge and reconnect with the natural world.

Seasonal changes bring their own charm to the park, transforming its landscape throughout the year. In spring, the gardens burst into bloom, filling the air with the scent of jasmine and lavender. Summer's long days draw people to the shaded groves and cool fountains, while autumn paints the trees in shades of gold and crimson. Even in winter, the park retains its beauty, with misty mornings and the bare branches of trees creating a serene, almost ethereal atmosphere. Each season offers a different perspective on Villa Doria Pamphili, ensuring that no two visits are ever quite the same.

Cultural events and activities occasionally animate the park, adding an extra layer of vibrancy to its already dynamic character. Outdoor concerts, art exhibitions, and festivals take advantage of the park's natural beauty and historical backdrop, creating memorable experiences for those who attend. These events are a reminder of the park's role as a communal space, a place where people come together to celebrate, create, and share in the joys of life.

Despite its many attractions, Villa Doria Pamphili remains something of a hidden gem, especially for visitors who tend to focus on Rome's more famous landmarks. Its location outside the city center means it is often overlooked in favor of sites like the Colosseum, the Vatican, or the Trevi Fountain. Yet for those willing to venture a bit further afield, the park offers a side of Rome that is peaceful, unhurried, and deeply rewarding. It is a place where you can experience the city's history and culture in a setting that feels removed from the hustle and bustle of urban life.

Practical considerations can enhance your visit to Villa Doria Pamphili. The park is easily accessible by public transport, with buses and trams connecting it to the city center. Comfortable walking shoes are a must, as the park's size and terrain require a fair amount of walking to fully appreciate. Bringing a picnic is a popular option, as the park's open spaces and scenic spots provide ideal settings for outdoor dining. For those who prefer a more leisurely experience, benches and shaded areas are plentiful, allowing you to sit and take in the beauty of your surroundings.

Villa Doria Pamphili is more than just a park; it is a living testament to Rome's ability to balance history, nature, and modern life. It is a place where the grandeur of the past meets the simplicity of the present, where the beauty of the natural world is complemented by the elegance of human craftsmanship. Whether you are a history buff, an art enthusiast, a nature lover, or simply someone looking for a moment of peace, the park offers something that speaks to the soul. Its vast, varied landscape invites you to explore, reflect, and lose yourself in its timeless charm, leaving you with memories that linger long after you've returned to the city streets.

CHAPTER 4: EXPLORING ROME'S ART AND ARCHITECTURE

Baroque Marvels: Bernini and Borromini's Masterpieces

The Baroque era in Rome was a time of dramatic transformation, when art and architecture reached new heights of emotional power, technical innovation, and sheer spectacle. In no small part, this vision was shaped by two of its most brilliant and contrasting figures: Gian Lorenzo Bernini and Francesco Borromini. These two architects and artists, often seen as rivals, left an indelible mark on the Eternal City, creating works that continue to captivate and inspire. Their masterpieces, though born of the same Baroque spirit, reflect distinctly different approaches to design and storytelling, embodying the tension and energy that defined the period.

Bernini, often called the "Michelangelo of his age," was a prodigy whose talents spanned sculpture, architecture, and even theater. His works are imbued with a sense of movement and emotion that draws the viewer into the drama of the scene. His vision for Baroque Rome was one of grandeur and theatricality, using space and light to create an almost cinematic effect. Borromini, on the other hand, was an innovator who challenged traditional forms and pushed the boundaries of architectural design. Where Bernini sought to awe and delight, Borromini sought to intrigue and provoke, using geometry and spatial manipulation to create buildings that were as intellectually stimulating as they were visually striking.

One of Bernini's most celebrated works is the Baldacchino in St. Peter's Basilica, a monumental bronze canopy that rises over the high altar and the tomb of St. Peter. Commissioned by Pope Urban VIII, the Baldacchino was designed to establish a visual focal point within the vast interior of the basilica, tying the altar to the soaring dome above. The structure is a masterpiece of symbolism and craftsmanship, with its twisting, vine-covered columns evoking the ancient Solomonic columns said to have adorned the Temple of Jerusalem. At the same time, the gilded bronze bees and suns—emblems of the Barberini family, to which Urban VIII belonged—assert the pope's authority and divine mandate. The Baldacchino's scale and intricate detail exemplify Bernini's ability to combine the monumental with the intimate, creating a work that is both overwhelming in its grandeur and deeply personal in its devotional intent.

Borromini's response to the grandeur of St. Peter's Basilica can be found in his masterpiece, San Carlo alle Quattro Fontane, a small church tucked away on a corner of the Quirinal Hill. Known affectionately as "San Carlino" due to its modest size, the church is a marvel of architectural ingenuity. Borromini's genius is evident in the undulating façade, where concave and convex forms create a sense of movement and fluidity that defies the rigidity of traditional classical design. Inside, the oval dome, adorned with a delicate geometric pattern of coffers, seems to float weightlessly above the nave, its lightness enhanced by the hidden windows that illuminate it from below. San Carlino is a testament to Borromini's ability to do more with less, creating a space that feels expansive and dynamic despite its physical constraints.

The rivalry between Bernini and Borromini is perhaps most evident in their respective contributions to Piazza Navona, one of Rome's most iconic public spaces. Bernini's Fountain of the Four Rivers, located at the center of the piazza, is a tour de force of sculptural and architectural integration. The fountain features four colossal figures representing the great rivers of the known continents—the Nile, the Ganges, the Danube, and the Rio de la Plata—each accompanied by symbolic animals and plants. The figures are arranged around a central obelisk, which rises dramatically from the fountain's base, creating a vertical axis that draws the eye upward. The dynamic poses and expressive gestures of the figures convey a sense of movement and vitality, transforming the fountain into a living tableau.

Borromini's contribution to Piazza Navona is the Church of Sant'Agnese in Agone, which stands directly opposite Bernini's fountain. The church's curving façade, with its twin bell towers and central dome, is a masterpiece of Baroque design, its rhythms and proportions carefully calibrated to create a sense of unity and balance. Inside, the church is equally impressive, with its soaring dome and richly decorated chapels. While Bernini's fountain celebrates the triumph of divine providence over the chaos of nature, Borromini's church invites contemplation and introspection, its serene interior providing a counterpoint to the drama of the piazza.

Perhaps the most famous anecdote about the rivalry between Bernini and Borromini involves the Fountain of the Four Rivers and Sant'Agnese in Agone. According to legend, Bernini sculpted the figure representing the Rio de la Plata with one arm raised as if to shield himself from the church, implying his disdain for Borromini's design. In response, Borromini supposedly positioned a statue of Saint Agnes on the church façade with a gesture of reassurance, as if to calm the fears of the fountain's figure. While this story is almost certainly apocryphal, it captures the enduring fascination with the dynamic between these two great artists.

One of Bernini's most personal and evocative works is the Ecstasy of Saint Teresa, located in the Cornaro Chapel of Santa Maria della Vittoria. This sculptural group depicts a moment of mystical rapture experienced by Saint Teresa of Ávila, as described in her writings. The saint is shown reclining on a cloud, her face contorted in an expression of divine ecstasy, while an angel stands above her, poised to pierce her heart with a golden arrow. The scene is illuminated by a hidden window that casts light onto the figures, heightening the sense of the supernatural. The surrounding architecture, with its theatrical arrangement of columns and gilded rays, transforms the chapel into a stage, drawing the viewer into the drama of the moment.

Borromini's approach to sacred architecture can be seen in Sant'Ivo alla Sapienza, a small church located within the courtyard of the University of Rome. The church's spiral lantern, which rises above the dome, is one of the most distinctive features of Baroque architecture, its dynamic form symbolizing the ascent of the soul toward God. Inside, the church's star-shaped plan and intricate geometry create a space that is both harmonious and intellectually stimulating. Sant'Ivo exemplifies Borromini's ability to infuse his designs with a sense of spiritual and mathematical order, reflecting his belief in the divine harmony of the universe.

Despite their differences, Bernini and Borromini shared a common goal: to create works that inspired awe and devotion. Their masterpieces, though distinct in style and approach, are united by their ability to engage the viewer on multiple levels, combining visual splendor with emotional and intellectual depth. Together, they shaped the identity of Baroque Rome, transforming the city into a living gallery of their genius.

Their influence extends far beyond Rome, inspiring generations of architects and artists who sought to capture the spirit of the Baroque. Bernini's ability to fuse sculpture and architecture into a seamless whole set a new standard for artistic integration, while Borromini's daring innovations in form and space opened new possibilities for architectural expression. Their works continue to draw millions of visitors to Rome each year, offering a glimpse into a world where art and architecture were not merely functional but profoundly transformative.

Exploring the masterpieces of Bernini and Borromini is an essential part of understanding Rome's Baroque legacy. Their works are more than monuments to individual genius; they are expressions of a city and a culture that sought to inspire, to challenge, and to elevate. Whether through the dynamic energy of Bernini's sculptures or the intricate geometry of Borromini's churches, these artists invite us to see the world through their eyes—a world where beauty, emotion, and intellect converge in perfect harmony.

Renaissance Rome: Michelangelo's Influence

Michelangelo Buonarroti was more than a master artist; he was a force that shaped the very fabric of Renaissance Rome. His influence extended beyond the boundaries of sculpture and painting, altering the city's artistic identity and redefining how art interacted with space, architecture, and human emotion. In a period marked by a cultural rebirth, Michelangelo's genius stood unparalleled, and his works became milestones in Rome's transformation into the epicenter of Renaissance art and thought. His fingerprints remain evident, from the Sistine Chapel's ceiling to the grandeur of St. Peter's Basilica, making him one of the most significant figures in the history of the Eternal City.

Arriving in Rome for the first time in 1496, Michelangelo was a young artist with immense promise but without the towering reputation he would later achieve. It was in this city that his talent found the ideal stage—a place where the ambitions of the papacy and the wealth of powerful patrons created an insatiable demand for the extraordinary. One of his earliest commissions in Rome was the Pietà, a sculpture that even today continues to leave viewers awestruck. Housed in St. Peter's Basilica, the Pietà depicts the Virgin Mary cradling the lifeless body of Christ. Michelangelo infused the marble with an emotional depth and meticulous detail that had never been seen before. The folds of Mary's robes seem to ripple like fabric, and the delicacy of Christ's body exudes both fragility and grace. This work not only launched his career but also introduced a new level of realism and humanity to religious art, setting a benchmark for all who followed.

Beyond the Pietà, Michelangelo's influence in Rome reached its zenith with his work on the Sistine Chapel. Commissioned by Pope Julius II in 1508, the task of painting the chapel's ceiling was both monumental and daunting. Michelangelo, primarily a sculptor, initially resisted the commission, but his eventual acceptance led to one of the most iconic achievements in art history. Over four years of backbreaking labor, Michelangelo transformed the ceiling into a visual masterpiece that depicted the story of Genesis, from the Creation of the World to the Fall of Man. The Creation of Adam, with its iconic image of God reaching out to touch Adam's hand, has become one of the most recognizable images in Western art. The ceiling's dynamic compositions, vivid colors, and anatomical precision revealed Michelangelo's mastery of both form and narrative. More than that, it elevated the Sistine Chapel from a place of worship to an immersive spiritual and artistic experience. Visitors to the chapel found themselves transported, their eyes drawn upward into a celestial realm that seemed alive with divine energy.

The ceiling of the Sistine Chapel displayed Michelangelo's unparalleled ability to blend technical skill with profound storytelling, but his relationship with the chapel was far from over. Decades later, he returned to paint The Last Judgment on the altar wall, a work that reflected not only his artistic evolution but also his spiritual concerns. In contrast to the ceiling's celebratory tone, The Last Judgment is a darker, more introspective piece, portraying the final reckoning of souls in vivid and often unsettling detail. Christ stands at the center, a commanding figure surrounded by the saved and the damned, their fates rendered with harrowing intensity. The work was controversial in its time for its unflinching depiction of nudity and its stark portrayal of divine justice, but it remains one of the most powerful expressions of

Michelangelo's vision. Together, the ceiling and the altar wall form a dialogue between creation and judgment, encapsulating the breadth of the human experience.

Michelangelo's impact on Renaissance Rome extended beyond his paintings and sculptures; he was also a visionary architect. His work on St. Peter's Basilica, though not completed during his lifetime, shaped the structure into the iconic building it is today. Appointed as chief architect in 1546, Michelangelo inherited a project that had already seen contributions from some of the greatest architects of the era, including Bramante and Raphael. His genius lay in his ability to unify their disparate plans, creating a cohesive design that emphasized both grandeur and harmony. One of his most significant contributions was the redesign of the basilica's dome, which remains one of the most recognizable features of the Roman skyline. Michelangelo's dome was an engineering marvel, combining classical proportions with innovative structural techniques to create a sense of both solidity and ascension. Its sweeping curves and intricate details embody the ideals of the Renaissance, where art, science, and faith converged.

While Michelangelo's work on St. Peter's Basilica is often celebrated for its monumental scale, his architectural genius is also evident in smaller, more intimate projects. One such example is the Piazza del Campidoglio, a public square on Rome's Capitoline Hill. Commissioned by Pope Paul III, Michelangelo reimagined the space as a harmonious interplay of architecture and urban planning. He designed a trapezoidal piazza flanked by three palaces, with a magnificent staircase leading up to the square and an equestrian statue of Marcus Aurelius at its center. The layout of the piazza subtly manipulates perspective, creating a sense of balance and order that draws visitors into the space. Michelangelo's design transformed the Capitoline Hill from a neglected area into a symbol of civic pride and cultural renewal, further cementing his role as a shaper of Rome's identity.

Michelangelo's influence on Renaissance Rome was not limited to his completed works; his ideas and innovations inspired countless artists and architects who followed. His ability to imbue stone and paint with life, his mastery of human anatomy, and his exploration of complex emotional and spiritual themes set new standards for artistic excellence. He challenged traditional boundaries, proving that art could be both intellectually rigorous and deeply moving. In the process, he redefined what it meant to be an artist, elevating the profession to one of intellectual and creative leadership.

Despite his towering achievements, Michelangelo's time in Rome was not without its challenges. He often found himself at odds with his patrons, navigating the complex politics of the papal court while wrestling with his own perfectionism. His letters and writings reveal a man who was both deeply committed to his work and profoundly aware of its demands. Yet, it was this relentless pursuit of excellence that enabled him to create works that continue to resonate across centuries.

Today, Michelangelo's legacy in Rome is inescapable. His works are not merely historical artifacts; they are living testaments to the power of human creativity and the enduring impact of the Renaissance. Visitors to the city can trace his influence from the Vatican to the Capitoline Hill, experiencing firsthand the spaces and images that have shaped the way we think about art, faith, and beauty. Michelangelo's contributions to Renaissance Rome are more than a chapter in history—they are a continuing source of inspiration, reminding us of the heights that can be achieved when talent, vision, and determination converge.

Caravaggio's Masterpieces in Roman Churches

The legacy of Michelangelo Merisi da Caravaggio, one of the most innovative and controversial artists of the Baroque era, is deeply embedded in the fabric of Rome. His revolutionary approach to painting, characterized by dramatic contrasts of light and shadow (chiaroscuro) and an unflinching realism, transformed the art world and continues to captivate audiences centuries later. While Caravaggio's tumultuous life often overshadowed his work—marked by brawls, arrests, and exile—the masterpieces he left behind in Roman churches stand as enduring testaments to his genius. These paintings, created for sacred spaces, reveal his ability to bring biblical narratives to life with an intensity and humanity that few artists have ever matched. To view these works in their original contexts, nestled within the chapels and altars for which they were intended, is to experience Caravaggio's art as it was meant to be seen: raw, immediate, and profoundly moving.

One of Caravaggio's most iconic works can be found in the Contarelli Chapel of the Church of San Luigi dei Francesi, just a short walk from Piazza Navona. This chapel houses a triptych of paintings that depict scenes from the life of Saint Matthew, commissioned by the French cardinal Matteo Contarelli in the late 16th century. Among these, "The Calling of Saint Matthew" is perhaps the most famous and serves as a cornerstone of Caravaggio's revolutionary style. The painting captures the moment when Jesus calls Matthew, a tax collector, to follow him. The setting is not some ethereal or idealized space but a dimly lit tavern, its dark, smoky atmosphere pierced by a single beam of light that illuminates the figures. The light, symbolic of divine intervention, cuts through the scene with surgical precision, highlighting Matthew's astonished expression as he points to himself in disbelief. The figures are dressed in the garb of Caravaggio's own time, grounding the biblical story in the gritty reality of 16th-century Rome. This immediacy and relatability were hallmarks of Caravaggio's work, drawing viewers into the narrative and making the divine feel palpably close.

Flanking "The Calling of Saint Matthew" are two other masterpieces: "The Martyrdom of Saint Matthew" and "Saint Matthew and the Angel." In the former, Caravaggio stages the saint's violent death with unrelenting realism, capturing the chaos and terror of the moment. The composition is dynamic, with twisting bodies and frantic gestures that seem to spill out of the frame, pulling the viewer into the scene. "Saint Matthew and the Angel," by contrast, is a more contemplative work, depicting the saint in the act of writing his gospel, guided by an angel. The intimacy of their interaction, underscored by the tender gesture of the angel's hand, reflects Caravaggio's ability to convey profound emotion through subtle details. Together, these three paintings form a cohesive narrative that celebrates Matthew's journey from sinner to saint, illustrating the transformative power of faith.

A short distance from San Luigi dei Francesi lies the Church of Sant'Agostino, home to another of Caravaggio's masterpieces: "Madonna di Loreto," also known as the "Madonna of the Pilgrims." This painting, commissioned for the Cavaletti Chapel, caused a stir upon its unveiling due to its unconventional portrayal of the Virgin Mary and her devotees. Caravaggio depicts the Madonna and Child standing in the doorway of a simple, weathered house, their figures illuminated by a soft, golden light. At their feet kneel two pilgrims, their faces lined with age and hardship, their bare feet caked with dirt. This unvarnished realism scandalized some contemporaries, who felt that Caravaggio's choice to depict the sacred through such a humble lens was inappropriate. Yet it is precisely this humility that makes the painting so powerful. The Madonna is not a remote, otherworldly figure; she is a mother, tender and approachable, who meets the pilgrims in their suffering. The stark contrast between the divine light and the earthy details of the scene underscores Caravaggio's belief that the sacred could be found in the ordinary, a theme that runs through much of his work.

Perhaps the most visceral of Caravaggio's Roman church paintings can be found in the Cerasi Chapel of Santa Maria del Popolo, located at the northern edge of Piazza del Popolo. Here, two monumental works face each other across the chapel: "The Crucifixion of Saint Peter" and "The Conversion of Saint Paul." These paintings, created for Tiberio Cerasi, showcase Caravaggio's ability to convey drama and emotion with unparalleled intensity. In "The Crucifixion of Saint Peter," the saint is depicted at the moment of his martyrdom, nailed to a cross that is being hoisted into position. The composition is stark and unflinching, with Peter's weathered face and muscular body rendered in meticulous detail. The three executioners, their faces obscured or turned away, emphasize the anonymity and banality of violence, while the diagonal lines of the composition draw the viewer's eye inexorably toward the cross.

Opposite this work is "The Conversion of Saint Paul," a painting that captures the transformative moment when Saul of Tarsus is struck down by divine light on the road to Damascus. Unlike traditional depictions of the scene, which often include a host of angels or a dramatic skyline, Caravaggio strips the composition to its essentials. Paul lies sprawled on the ground, his arms outstretched in a gesture of surrender, while his horse and a stable hand dominate the foreground. The light that engulfs Paul is the only indication of the divine presence, a subtle yet powerful reminder of the invisible force at work. This minimalist approach heightens the emotional impact of the scene, focusing the viewer's attention on Paul's moment of spiritual awakening.

Caravaggio's works in Roman churches are not merely paintings; they are immersive experiences that engage the viewer on multiple levels. His use of light and shadow creates a sense of depth and movement, making the figures appear almost alive. His unflinching realism brings biblical narratives into the realm of human experience, bridging the gap between the sacred and the profane. These qualities make his paintings as relevant today as they were in his own time, offering a window into the human condition and the mysteries of faith.

The opportunity to view Caravaggio's masterpieces in their original settings is a privilege that few other cities can offer. Unlike works housed in museums, where the context is often divorced from the content, these paintings remain embedded in the spaces for which they were created. The interplay between the art, the architecture, and the liturgical function of the churches enhances the viewer's understanding of Caravaggio's vision. Whether it is the way the natural light filters through the chapel windows, casting subtle shadows on the paintings, or the quiet reverence of the spaces themselves, experiencing these works in situ adds a layer of depth and authenticity that cannot be replicated.

For those seeking to explore Caravaggio's legacy in Rome, a visit to these churches is both a journey through art history and a profound encounter with the artist's genius. Each painting offers a glimpse into Caravaggio's world, a world where light and darkness, grace and sin, humanity and divinity collide. His ability to capture the essence of the human spirit, with all its flaws and aspirations, ensures that his works continue to resonate across time and space. In the quiet chapels of San Luigi dei Francesi, Sant'Agostino, and Santa Maria del Popolo, Caravaggio's art speaks to us still, a testament to the enduring power of his vision.

Contemporary Art in the Eternal City

Rome's identity is often tied to its ancient ruins, Renaissance masterpieces, and Baroque splendor, but beneath its historical layers lies a vibrant and evolving contemporary art scene. The

Eternal City, long associated with the grandeur of the past, now serves as a canvas for modern creativity and a hub for contemporary artists who draw inspiration from its rich history while forging new paths. From cutting-edge galleries and experimental art spaces to public installations that transform the urban landscape, Rome's contemporary art scene is a dynamic counterpoint to its storied traditions. It's a testament to the city's ability to embrace modernity without losing touch with its heritage, showing that art in Rome is not just about looking back but also about innovating, challenging, and reimagining the future.

The MAXXI—Museo Nazionale delle Arti del XXI Secolo—is a cornerstone of contemporary art in Rome. Designed by Iraqi-British architect Zaha Hadid, the museum is itself a work of art, with its bold, fluid lines and interplay of curves and angles offering a stark contrast to the classical architecture that dominates the city. Opened in 2010, MAXXI is dedicated to contemporary art and architecture, housing an ever-growing collection of works by some of the most influential artists and architects of the 21st century. The museum's exhibitions range from multimedia installations and experimental photography to large-scale sculptures and conceptual art, reflecting the diversity and vitality of the contemporary art world. Its permanent collection includes works by artists such as Anish Kapoor, William Kentridge, and Gerhard Richter, while its temporary exhibitions often explore themes at the intersection of art, technology, and social issues. Walking through MAXXI's halls, visitors are reminded that Rome is not a city frozen in time but one that continues to evolve and respond to the challenges and opportunities of the modern era.

One of the most intriguing aspects of Rome's contemporary art scene is its ability to integrate modern works into the fabric of the city. Public art installations and street art have become increasingly prominent, transforming Rome's streets, squares, and even neglected corners into open-air galleries. The Ostiense and Testaccio districts, once industrial areas, have become hotspots for street art, with large-scale murals and graffiti adding bursts of color and creativity to the urban landscape. Artists such as Blu, Jorit, and Alice Pasquini have left their mark on these neighborhoods, using walls and buildings as their canvases to address topics ranging from social justice and politics to personal narratives and cultural identity. These works not only beautify the city but also challenge viewers to engage with contemporary issues, creating a dialogue between the art and its audience.

Another key player in Rome's contemporary art scene is the Galleria Nazionale d'Arte Moderna e Contemporanea (GNAM), located near the Villa Borghese gardens. While the gallery's collection spans the 19th and 20th centuries, it has increasingly embraced contemporary art, offering a platform for both Italian and international artists. GNAM's expansive spaces allow for bold and ambitious exhibitions, including large-scale installations, video art, and interactive works. The gallery's commitment to contemporary art is evident in its partnerships with global institutions and its efforts to support emerging artists through residencies and commissions. A visit to GNAM provides a comprehensive overview of how contemporary art has evolved in dialogue with the past, bridging the gap between tradition and innovation.

Independent galleries and art spaces also play a crucial role in fostering contemporary art in Rome. These venues, often tucked away in unexpected corners of the city, serve as incubators for experimental and avant-garde projects. Galleria Lorcan O'Neill, located in a converted stable in Trastevere, is one such space. Known for its minimalist aesthetic, the gallery showcases works by internationally renowned artists such as Tracey Emin, Kiki Smith, and Martin Creed, as well as emerging talents. Its intimate setting allows for a close and personal engagement with the art, creating an environment where visitors can reflect and connect with the works on display.

Another standout is Pastificio Cerere, a former pasta factory in the San Lorenzo district that has been transformed into a multidisciplinary art center. The space is home to artists' studios, galleries, and cultural events, fostering a sense of community and collaboration among creatives. Pastificio Cerere's exhibitions often push the boundaries of conventional art, exploring themes like identity, memory, and the relationship between art and technology. Its industrial setting, with its exposed brick walls and steel beams, provides a striking backdrop for contemporary works, emphasizing the dialogue between tradition and modernity that defines Rome's art scene.

The rise of contemporary art fairs and festivals has further cemented Rome's status as a hub for modern creativity. Events like Romaeuropa Festival, which spans multiple disciplines including visual arts, theater, and music, showcase the city's commitment to cultural innovation. These events bring together artists, curators, and collectors from around the world, creating opportunities for exchange and collaboration. They also provide a platform for emerging artists to gain visibility, ensuring that the next generation of creatives has a voice in shaping the city's cultural landscape.

Rome's contemporary art scene is not confined to galleries and museums; it extends into the digital realm as well. The city has embraced new technologies, with artists using virtual reality, augmented reality, and digital installations to create immersive experiences. Institutions like the Digital Art Festival and Spazio Nuovo have spearheaded initiatives that explore the intersection of art and technology, challenging traditional notions of what art can be. These innovations reflect a broader trend in contemporary art, where boundaries are increasingly blurred, and the medium becomes as important as the message.

The intersection of contemporary art and Rome's historical heritage is perhaps one of the most compelling aspects of the city's cultural scene. Projects like the Rome Art Week and the Biennale Arte Contemporanea di Roma have sought to create a dialogue between past and present, using ancient sites as venues for modern art installations. For example, the ruins of the Baths of Caracalla have hosted contemporary sculptures and installations that interact with the massive stone structures, creating a juxtaposition that highlights both the timelessness of art and the passage of time. These projects challenge viewers to see history not as static but as something that continues to inspire and inform the present.

Despite its growing prominence, contemporary art in Rome faces challenges, particularly when it comes to funding and public support. Many artists and galleries operate on limited budgets, relying on private patrons and international collaborations to sustain their work. However, these challenges have also fostered a sense of resilience and ingenuity within the community. Artists and curators have found creative ways to engage with the public, from pop-up exhibitions and art walks to social media campaigns that bring art into the digital age. This adaptability ensures that Rome's contemporary art scene remains vibrant and accessible, even in the face of economic and logistical constraints.

For visitors, exploring contemporary art in Rome offers a unique perspective on the city. It's an opportunity to see how artists respond to the legacy of the past while addressing the complexities of the modern world. Whether it's standing before a monumental mural in Ostiense, wandering through the futuristic halls of MAXXI, or discovering a hidden gallery in a cobblestoned alley, engaging with contemporary art in Rome is an experience that challenges, inspires, and enriches. It's a reminder that the Eternal City is not just a museum of history but a living, breathing organism that continues to grow and evolve, shaped by the creativity and vision of those who call it home.

The Beauty of Roman Fountains

The fountains of Rome are more than just sources of water; they are vessels of history, art, and engineering that have transformed public spaces into displays of grandeur and ingenuity over centuries. Scattered throughout the city, these fountains are among Rome's most iconic features, weaving together the aesthetics of ancient Rome, the Renaissance, and the Baroque periods. They evoke a sense of wonder not only because of their beauty but also because of the stories they tell—stories of emperors, popes, artists, and engineers who sought to bring life and vitality to the city through these flowing masterpieces. To walk through Rome is to encounter these fountains at every turn, each one a reflection of its era, its patrons, and the ambitions of the time.

The origins of Rome's fountains are deeply tied to the city's ancient aqueduct system, a marvel of engineering that supplied fresh water to its citizens. By the time of the Roman Empire, an intricate network of aqueducts carried water across great distances, feeding baths, households, and public fountains. These fountains were not merely functional; they were symbols of Roman prosperity and technological prowess. The Aqua Virgo, one of the ancient aqueducts still in use today, dates back to 19 BCE and continues to supply water to some of Rome's most famous fountains, including the iconic Trevi Fountain. The survival of these ancient systems underscores the durability of Roman engineering and provides a direct link between the city's past and present.

The Trevi Fountain, completed in 1762, is perhaps the most famous fountain in the world and a quintessential example of Baroque art. Designed by Nicola Salvi and completed by Giuseppe Pannini, the fountain is a theatrical spectacle of water, stone, and sculpture. Its central figure is Oceanus, the god of water, who stands triumphantly on a chariot pulled by sea horses, flanked by allegorical figures representing abundance and health. The cascading water, which seems to bring the sculptures to life, flows into a large basin, creating a mesmerizing interplay of sound and movement. The fountain's location, at the terminus of the Aqua Virgo, adds to its historical significance, connecting it to the ancient Roman tradition of celebrating water as a life-giving force. Of course, no visit to the Trevi Fountain is complete without the ritual of tossing a coin over one's shoulder—a tradition said to ensure a return to Rome.

While the Trevi Fountain embodies the grandeur of the Baroque period, the Fountain of the Four Rivers in Piazza Navona represents the creative genius of Gian Lorenzo Bernini. Commissioned by Pope Innocent X in 1651, this fountain is a masterful blend of sculpture and architecture, designed to symbolize the universality of the Catholic Church. The fountain features four colossal figures representing the great rivers of the four continents known at the time: the Nile, the Ganges, the Danube, and the Rio de la Plata. Each figure is accompanied by symbolic flora and fauna, creating a vivid tableau that captures the viewer's imagination. Rising above the figures is an ancient Egyptian obelisk, a nod to Rome's imperial past and its role as a custodian of history. The Fountain of the Four Rivers is not merely a decorative feature; it is a statement of power, faith, and artistic innovation, encapsulating the spirit of Baroque Rome.

The Renaissance period also left its mark on Rome's fountains, emphasizing harmony, proportion, and a revival of classical ideals. One of the most notable examples is the Fountain of the Turtle, or Fontana delle Tartarughe, located in the quiet Piazza Mattei. Designed by Giacomo della Porta and later modified by Taddeo Landini, the fountain features four bronze youths gracefully supporting marble basins, with water flowing delicately from their hands. The turtles, which give the fountain its name, were added later and lend a whimsical charm to the composition. Unlike the monumental fountains of the Baroque period, the Fountain of the Turtle exudes intimacy and elegance, reflecting the humanist ideals of the Renaissance.

Rome's fountains are not confined to its historic center; they are found in every neighborhood, each with its own character and significance. The Fountain of the Naiads in Piazza della Repubblica, for example, is a striking example of late 19th-century design. Its sensual and dynamic figures, representing water nymphs, caused controversy when it was unveiled but have since become a beloved symbol of modern Rome. The fountain's circular design and its position in a busy piazza make it a focal point of urban life, a place where the energy of the city converges.

Many of Rome's fountains were commissioned by popes, who saw them as a way to both beautify the city and demonstrate their power and benevolence. Pope Sixtus V, in particular, was a prolific patron of fountains, overseeing the construction of the Fontana dell'Acqua Felice, also known as the Fountain of Moses. This monumental fountain marks the terminus of the Acqua Felice aqueduct, one of the first to be restored in the post-Classical era. Its central figure, a larger-than-life Moses, stands flanked by bas-reliefs depicting scenes from the Old Testament. The fountain's design, while criticized by some for its heavy-handed proportions, reflects the Counter-Reformation's emphasis on conveying religious messages through art.

The relationship between Rome's fountains and its aqueducts is a fascinating story of continuity and adaptation. While many of the ancient aqueducts fell into disrepair during the Middle Ages, the Renaissance and Baroque periods saw a renewed interest in restoring these systems. The Aqua Paola, for instance, was rebuilt in the 17th century to supply water to the Janiculum Hill and the Fontana dell'Acqua Paola, a grand fountain also known as Il Fontanone. This fountain, with its cascading waterfalls and triumphant arches, is a celebration of the engineering feats that made Rome's fountains possible.

Standing before it, one can almost hear the echoes of ancient Rome, where water was not just a necessity but a source of pride and identity.

Rome's fountains are as much about the sensory experience as they are about visual beauty. The sound of water flowing over stone creates a calming backdrop to the city's bustling streets, offering moments of serenity in an otherwise chaotic environment. Whether it's the gentle trickle of a small neighborhood fountain or the roaring cascades of a monumental one, the soundscape of Rome is defined by its fountains. On hot summer days, the cool mist rising from these waters provides a welcome respite, drawing people to their edges to rest, reflect, or simply enjoy the view.

The fountains also serve as gathering places, where locals and tourists alike come together, bridging the gap between history and everyday life. In Piazza Navona, children play around the fountains while artists set up their easels nearby, capturing the scene in paint. At the Trevi Fountain, couples pose for photographs, their faces lit with joy as they participate in a tradition that has spanned generations. These moments of connection, facilitated by the presence of fountains, highlight their role as social and cultural hubs.

In the modern era, Rome continues to preserve and celebrate its fountains while also exploring new interpretations of this age-old tradition. Contemporary artists and designers have created fountains that blend innovation with respect for the past, adding new layers to the city's rich tapestry. These modern works, though fewer in number, ensure that the tradition of fountain-making remains alive, evolving alongside the city it serves.

The beauty of Rome's fountains lies not only in their artistry but also in their integration into the life of the city. They are not isolated monuments but living, breathing parts of Rome's identity, connecting its ancient past to its vibrant present. Each fountain tells a story—of the people who built it, the era it represents, and the role it continues to play in the daily rhythms of the city. To experience Rome is to experience its fountains, to stand before them and feel the pulse of history flowing through their waters. They are, in every sense, the lifeblood of the Eternal City.

Rome's Obelisks: Ancient Egypt in Italy

The obelisks of Rome are among the most fascinating testaments to the city's layered history, standing as silent witnesses to the blending of two of the most influential civilizations of the ancient world: Egypt and Rome. These towering monoliths, with their sharp spires and enigmatic hieroglyphs, are not merely decorative marvels; they are symbols of conquest, cultural exchange, and the enduring allure of the past. Transported from the deserts of Egypt or carved anew in Rome itself, they have become an intrinsic part of the Eternal City's landscape, seamlessly integrating the mystique of the Nile Valley with the grandeur of the Roman Empire. Their presence in piazzas and squares throughout the city is not only a reminder of Rome's imperial power but also a reflection of its deep admiration for and appropriation of foreign traditions.

The story of how these obelisks came to dot Rome begins with the Roman conquest of Egypt in 30 BCE, following the defeat of Cleopatra and Mark Antony by Octavian, who would later become Emperor Augustus. With Egypt transformed into a Roman province, its treasures became spoils of war, and among the most prized were its obelisks. These objects, steeped in religious and cultural significance, were seen as trophies of imperial domination and symbols of Rome's ability to absorb the grandeur of other civilizations into its own. Augustus, in particular, played a pivotal role in initiating the transport of obelisks to Rome, setting a precedent that would be followed by his successors. The first such monument he brought was the Obelisk of Montecitorio, originally erected in the Egyptian city of Heliopolis during the reign of Pharaoh Psamtik II. In Rome, it was repurposed as a gnomon for a massive sundial, its shadow marking the passage of time in the newly established Campus Martius.

Another obelisk brought to Rome by Augustus now stands in the Piazza del Popolo, towering over the square as a testament to the emperor's vision. Known as the Flaminio Obelisk, it, too, originated in Heliopolis and dates back to the reigns of Seti I and Ramses II. Its hieroglyphs, though weathered by time, still sing praises to the gods of ancient Egypt, creating a striking juxtaposition with its current Christian surroundings. The decision to place such an overtly foreign object in a prominent public space speaks to Rome's unique approach to cultural assimilation. Rather than suppressing the identities of the peoples they conquered, the Romans often celebrated and integrated their achievements, using them to enhance their own prestige.

The transport of these massive obelisks from Egypt to Rome was no small feat, requiring incredible ingenuity and resources. These monoliths, often weighing hundreds of tons, were first dismantled and then loaded onto specially constructed ships capable of navigating the Mediterranean. The voyage itself was fraught with challenges, as the sheer weight of the cargo made the vessels vulnerable to storms and other hazards. Upon arrival in Rome, the obelisks had to be carefully unloaded and transported to their designated locations, a task that involved an intricate system of pulleys, ropes, and manpower. The engineering expertise required for such an endeavor is a testament to the Romans' unparalleled ability to adapt and innovate.

While Augustus initiated the trend of relocating obelisks to Rome, subsequent emperors continued the practice, each leaving their own mark on the city's skyline. Caligula, the infamous and controversial ruler, brought the Vatican Obelisk to Rome, originally placing it in the Circus of Nero. This obelisk, which now stands in St. Peter's Square, is unique in that it lacks hieroglyphic inscriptions, leading some to speculate that it was left unfinished in Egypt. Its relocation to its current position during the Renaissance was a monumental undertaking overseen by Pope Sixtus V and the architect Domenico Fontana. The effort to move the obelisk from its original site to the square required months of planning and the labor of hundreds of workers, as well as an elaborate system of scaffolding and winches. The event was so significant that the pope declared a day of public fasting and prayer to ensure its success.

Perhaps the most ambitious display of Rome's love affair with obelisks came during the reign of Emperor Domitian, who commissioned the construction of new obelisks in the Egyptian style. These Rome-made obelisks were often inscribed with Latin rather than hieroglyphs, reflecting a synthesis of Roman and Egyptian traditions. One such example is the Obelisk of Domitian, now located outside the church of Santa Maria sopra Minerva. Carved from red granite and adorned with Latin inscriptions glorifying the emperor, it demonstrates how the Romans reimagined obelisks not just as artifacts of conquest but as symbols of their own imperial ideology.

The Christianization of Rome in the fourth century CE marked a turning point in the history of its obelisks. As pagan symbols, many of these monuments fell into disuse or were toppled and buried, their significance obscured by the rise of a new religious order. However, the Renaissance brought a renewed interest in the classical past, and the obelisks were rediscovered, excavated, and restored to their former glory. Popes of the Renaissance and Baroque periods, eager to assert their authority and align themselves with Rome's imperial legacy, incorporated obelisks into their urban renewal projects. Pope Sixtus V, in particular, was instrumental in repositioning obelisks in key locations throughout the city, creating axial alignments and visual connections between churches, basilicas, and public spaces. His vision transformed the obelisks into Christian symbols, often surmounted by crosses or other religious emblems, thereby recontextualizing them within the framework of the Counter-Reformation.

Modern visitors to Rome can experience the majesty of these obelisks in a variety of settings, each offering a unique perspective on their historical and cultural significance. The Lateran Obelisk, for example, is the tallest in Rome and one of the oldest, dating back to the reign of Pharaoh Thutmose III. Originally erected in Karnak, it was brought to Rome by Emperor Constantius II in the fourth century and placed in the Circus Maximus. Today, it stands in the Piazza di San Giovanni in Laterano, its towering presence a reminder of its journey across time and continents.

The Piazza Navona is another must-visit site for obelisk enthusiasts, where Bernini's Fountain of the Four Rivers serves as the base for the Agonalis Obelisk. This particular obelisk, while smaller than others in the city, is a prime example of how Roman and Egyptian elements were blended to create new artistic expressions. Its hieroglyphs, though largely decorative rather than authentic, evoke the mysticism of ancient Egypt, while its placement atop Bernini's dynamic sculpture underscores its role as a focal point of Baroque urban design.

The enduring appeal of Rome's obelisks lies in their ability to connect disparate eras and cultures. They are, at once, relics of ancient Egypt, trophies of the Roman Empire, symbols of Christian triumph, and icons of Renaissance and Baroque artistry. Each obelisk tells a story, not just of its creation and original purpose but also of its journey to Rome and its transformation within the city's ever-changing cultural and political landscape. To stand before one of these monoliths is to glimpse the complexities of history, to feel the weight of centuries in a single gaze.

Rome's obelisks are more than monuments; they are bridges between worlds. They remind us of the interconnectedness of human civilizations, the ways in which art and architecture transcend boundaries to inspire and endure. As they rise above the piazzas and streets of the Eternal City, they invite us to reflect on the power of cultural exchange and the lasting impact of the past on the present. In their silent permanence, they speak volumes, urging us to look up and consider the stories they carry.

CHAPTER 5: ROME'S CULINARY SCENE

Traditional Roman Dishes You Must Try

Roman cuisine is a reflection of its city—simple yet sophisticated, steeped in history, and bursting with character. It is a culinary tradition rooted in centuries of resourcefulness, where humble ingredients are transformed into unforgettable dishes through techniques refined over generations. Whether served in a bustling trattoria, a quiet osteria, or cooked in a Roman kitchen, the flavors tell stories of shepherds, farmers, and city dwellers alike. To taste Rome is to taste a history both rich and unpretentious, where every bite carries the essence of the Eternal City. For anyone visiting Rome, sampling its traditional dishes is an essential part of understanding its culture, its people, and its way of life.

Cacio e pepe is the epitome of Roman simplicity, yet its perfection relies on precision. Translating to "cheese and pepper," this dish is a masterclass in doing more with less. Thick strands of tonnarelli pasta are coated in a silky sauce made only from Pecorino Romano cheese, freshly cracked black pepper, and the starchy water in which the pasta was boiled. The heat and timing are critical, as the cheese must melt into the pasta water to create a smooth emulsion without clumping. Its flavor is pure and intense, the sharpness of the Pecorino balancing the warmth of the pepper, making it a dish that lingers in your memory long after the last bite. Served in nearly every Roman eatery, cacio e pepe is a reminder that mastery of ingredients and technique is more powerful than an extensive list of components.

Carbonara is perhaps the most internationally famous Roman dish, but the authentic version is a revelation to those accustomed to imitations. Forget the cream or garlic often added in other countries; true Roman carbonara is a celebration of simplicity and richness. Made with guanciale (cured pork jowl), egg yolks, Pecorino Romano, black pepper, and pasta—usually spaghetti or rigatoni—it is a dish that demands careful attention to texture and balance. The guanciale is rendered until crisp, its fat providing the base for a creamy sauce created by the perfect combination of egg yolks and Pecorino. The pasta must be hot enough to cook the eggs gently but not so hot that they scramble. Each forkful is a harmony of salty, creamy, and savory elements, with the guanciale adding a smoky depth that elevates the dish beyond the ordinary.

Amatriciana, originating from the nearby town of Amatrice, has become an integral part of Roman culinary tradition. Its defining feature is its vibrant tomato-based sauce, enriched by the saltiness of guanciale and the sharpness of Pecorino Romano. Unlike many pasta dishes, amatriciana offers a bolder, tangier profile, with a hint of smokiness from the guanciale that complements the tartness of the tomatoes. Bucatini, a thick, hollow pasta, is traditionally used, its tubular shape perfect for holding onto the sauce. The dish is a celebration of robust flavors, and its origins as a shepherd's meal—designed to be hearty and satisfying—are evident in every bite. It is a dish that embodies the resourcefulness of Roman cuisine, where simple ingredients are elevated to greatness through careful preparation.

Gricia, often referred to as "carbonara without eggs" or "amatriciana without tomatoes," is a lesser-known but equally treasured dish in Roman kitchens. Dating back to a time before tomatoes were introduced to Italy, gricia is made with guanciale, Pecorino Romano, black pepper, and pasta. Its flavors are clean and focused, with the richness of the guanciale and the sharpness of the Pecorino creating a luxurious coating for the pasta. The absence of eggs or tomatoes allows the other ingredients to shine, making it a dish that is both understated and deeply satisfying. Gricia is a reminder of the historical roots of Roman cuisine, a connection to a time when dishes were crafted to make the most of the ingredients at hand.

Saltimbocca alla Romana is a dish that embodies the Roman approach to cooking: minimalism meets bold flavor. Thin slices of veal are topped with sage and prosciutto, then lightly sautéed in butter and white wine. The name "saltimbocca" translates to "jump in the mouth," a fitting description for the burst of flavor delivered by this dish. The veal is tender and juicy, the prosciutto adds a salty richness, and the sage provides a fragrant herbal note. The sauce, made from the pan juices, butter, and wine, ties everything together with a silky finish. Saltimbocca is a dish that feels indulgent yet effortless, a hallmark of Roman cookery.

Carciofi alla Romana, or Roman-style artichokes, highlight the city's love affair with this vegetable. Artichokes are cleaned, trimmed, and stuffed with a mixture of garlic, parsley, mint, and breadcrumbs before being braised in a mixture of water, olive oil, and white wine. The result is a tender, flavorful dish where the artichoke's natural sweetness is complemented by the aromatic stuffing. Served warm or at room temperature, carciofi alla Romana is a springtime favorite, showcasing the bounty of the season and the Roman talent for coaxing maximum flavor from simple ingredients.

Carciofi alla Giudia offers a completely different take on artichokes, showing the influence of Rome's Jewish community on its cuisine. This dish involves deep-frying whole artichokes until their leaves are crispy and golden, resembling a flower in full bloom. The outer leaves are crunchy and savory, while the heart remains tender and rich. The simplicity of the preparation belies the complexity of textures and flavors, making it a standout dish that is as visually striking as it is delicious. Found in the Roman Jewish neighborhood of the Ghetto, carciofi alla Giudia is a testament to the culinary contributions of the city's diverse communities.

Supplì, Rome's answer to the rice ball, is a street food staple that offers a taste of comfort and nostalgia. These deep-fried morsels are made by forming seasoned risotto (often flavored with tomato and meat sauce) around a core of mozzarella, then coating them in breadcrumbs and frying them to golden perfection. When bitten into, the mozzarella stretches like a string, earning them the nickname "supplì al telefono." Crispy on the outside, creamy and cheesy on the inside, supplì are a quintessential Roman snack, often enjoyed as an appetizer or a quick bite on the go.

Abbacchio alla Romana, or Roman-style lamb, is a dish steeped in tradition, often served during Easter celebrations. Tender cuts of young lamb are marinated in a mixture of garlic, rosemary, olive oil, and white wine before being roasted or braised to perfection. The result is a dish that is both succulent and aromatic, with the flavors of the marinade permeating the meat. Abbacchio alla Romana is a celebration of Roman hospitality, a dish meant to be shared with family and friends during special occasions.

Maritozzi, sweet brioche buns often filled with whipped cream, are a beloved Roman treat that bridges the gap between breakfast and dessert. These pillowy buns, lightly flavored with citrus zest, are a reminder of Rome's sweeter side. Traditionally eaten during Lent, maritozzi have become a year-round favorite, offering a moment of indulgence with a coffee in hand.

Roman cuisine is not merely about sustenance; it is an expression of the city's soul. It tells stories of its people, its history, and its enduring love for simple, honest food. Tasting these dishes is an intimate way of experiencing Rome, connecting with its traditions and savoring its essence. In every plate, there is a story waiting to be discovered, a flavor waiting to be remembered. These dishes are not just meals; they are a journey into the heart of Rome itself.

The Best Pizzerias and Gelaterias in Rome

Rome is a city where culinary traditions thrive, and two of its most beloved offerings—pizza and gelato—stand as testaments to its rich gastronomic culture. While pasta may reign supreme in the Roman culinary kingdom, locals and visitors alike often find themselves drawn to the simplicity and indulgence of a well-made pizza or a perfectly churned gelato. The Eternal City is home to an astounding variety of pizzerias and gelaterias, each offering a unique take on these staples of Italian cuisine. Finding the best spots to savor these treats is a journey in itself, a delicious exploration of Rome's neighborhoods and the artisans who dedicate their craft to perfecting these iconic foods.

Pizza in Rome is a different experience compared to other parts of Italy, particularly Naples. Roman pizza has its own distinctive characteristics: the crust is thin and crispy, often referred to as "scrocchiarella," with a delightful crunch that distinguishes it from the softer, chewier Neapolitan variety. The toppings are usually simple, allowing the quality of the ingredients to shine through. For a truly authentic Roman pizza experience, a visit to Pizzeria Da Remo in Testaccio is essential. This traditional pizzeria is a neighborhood institution, known for its no-frills atmosphere and high-quality pizzas. Their Margherita is a classic, with a perfectly balanced combination of tangy tomato sauce, creamy mozzarella, and fragrant basil on a crisp, charred crust. Another standout is the pizza bianca, a Roman specialty that skips the tomato sauce in favor of olive oil, rosemary, and coarse salt, creating a deceptively simple yet deeply flavorful dish.

For those seeking a modern twist on Roman pizza, Seu Pizza Illuminati in the Trastevere area offers a creative and contemporary approach. Helmed by chef Pier Daniele Seu, this pizzeria has gained a reputation for pushing the boundaries of traditional pizza-making while maintaining respect for its roots. The menu features inventive toppings such as smoked salmon and dill or mortadella with pistachios, as well as reimagined classics like their elevated quattro formaggi. The dough is a revelation—airy, light, and perfectly blistered from the high-temperature oven. The restaurant's sleek, modern design and impeccable service make it a favorite among both locals and tourists looking for a more refined pizza experience.

No discussion of Roman pizza would be complete without mentioning Pizzarium, the brainchild of renowned pizza al taglio (pizza by the slice) master Gabriele Bonci. Located near the Vatican, Pizzarium is a tiny, unassuming storefront that has achieved legendary status in the world of pizza. Bonci's creations are anything but ordinary—his dough is made with carefully sourced, stone-ground flours and fermented for up to 72 hours, resulting in a light, airy base with a tantalizing crunch. The toppings are seasonal, imaginative, and often sourced from small local producers. One slice might feature zucchini flowers and anchovies, while another could be topped with figs, prosciutto, and gorgonzola. Each slice is an explosion of flavor, and the ever-changing menu ensures that no two visits are the same.

As the sun sets over Rome, another pizza tradition comes to life: pinsa. Often considered a precursor to modern pizza, pinsa has been enjoying a resurgence in popularity in recent years. The dough, made from a blend of wheat, soy, and rice flour, is hydrated more than traditional pizza dough and fermented for a longer time, resulting in a light, crisp base with a tender center. La Pratolina, located in the Prati neighborhood, is one of the best places to try this ancient Roman specialty. Their pinsas come in a variety of flavors, from classics like margherita to more adventurous combinations like truffle cream with porcini mushrooms.

After indulging in pizza, a visit to one of Rome's many gelaterias is the perfect way to end a meal—or to enjoy a refreshing break during a day of sightseeing. Gelato in Rome is an art form, with each gelateria offering its own unique flavors and techniques. For a truly artisanal experience, Gelateria del Teatro is a must-visit. Nestled in a picturesque alley near Piazza Navona, this gelateria is known for its commitment to using high-quality, natural ingredients. Flavors like rosemary honey and lemon, ricotta with caramelized figs, and Sicilian pistachio showcase the creativity and passion of the gelato makers. Watching the gelato being churned in the open kitchen adds to the charm, making it an experience as well as a treat.

In the Trastevere neighborhood, Fatamorgana stands out for its innovative approach to gelato. The founder, Maria Agnese Spagnuolo, is a pioneer in creating unique flavor combinations that cater to a range of dietary needs, including vegan and gluten-free options. Flavors like basil with walnuts and honey, black rice with rose petals, and chocolate with Himalayan salt and black cardamom push the boundaries of traditional gelato while remaining balanced and delicious. The texture is consistently smooth and creamy, a testament to the meticulous attention to detail that goes into every batch.

For those looking for a more classic gelato experience, Giolitti is a Roman institution that has been serving gelato since 1900. Located near the Pantheon, this historic gelateria exudes old-world charm, with its marble counters and impeccably dressed staff. The flavors here are timeless, with staples like hazelnut, stracciatella, and tiramisu stealing the show. A signature touch is the dollop of whipped cream, or panna, added to each cone or cup at no extra cost. The richness of the gelato, paired with the creamy panna, is a match made in dessert heaven.

Another gem in the heart of Rome is Come il Latte, a gelateria that has built a loyal following for its ultra-creamy gelato and luxurious presentation. The name, which translates to "Like

Milk," reflects the emphasis on using fresh, high-quality milk as the foundation for their gelato. Flavors like Madagascar vanilla, salted caramel, and dark chocolate with orange zest are indulgent yet refined. The option to drizzle dark or white chocolate over your gelato before it is served adds an extra layer of decadence, making each visit feel like a special occasion.

For gelato purists, Otaleg in the Monteverde area is a revelation. The name, which is "gelato" spelled backward, hints at the playful yet serious approach taken by owner and gelato master Marco Radicioni. Otaleg is known for its commitment to sourcing the finest ingredients, from hazelnuts from Piedmont to lemons from Amalfi. The gelato is stored in covered stainless steel cylinders, ensuring optimal freshness and temperature. Flavors are intense and true to their ingredients, whether it's the deep, nutty richness of pistachio or the bright, tangy sweetness of wild strawberry.

Rome's pizzerias and gelaterias offer more than just food—they provide a sensory journey through the city's culture, history, and innovation. Each bite of pizza and each spoonful of gelato is a testament to the dedication and creativity of the artisans who make them. Whether you're savoring a simple slice of margherita in a bustling pizzeria or indulging in an adventurous gelato flavor on a quiet cobblestoned street, these experiences are an essential part of what makes Rome unforgettable. The city's culinary treasures remind us that food is not just sustenance—it is an expression of identity, a celebration of tradition, and a source of joy that lingers long after the last bite.

Wine and Aperitivo Culture: How to Drink Like a Roman

The culture of wine and aperitivo in Rome is not just about the act of drinking; it is a ritual, a way of life, and an integral part of social and culinary traditions. Romans have mastered the art of pairing fine wines with conviviality, and the pre-dinner aperitivo hour is a sacred time for unwinding, connecting with friends, and savoring small bites while sipping on perfectly selected beverages. To truly drink like a Roman, one must embrace the slow pace, the appreciation of quality over quantity, and the understanding that wine and aperitivo are as much about the people you share them with as they are about the flavors in your glass.

Wine has been a cornerstone of Roman culture since antiquity, with its history stretching back thousands of years to the days when the Roman Empire cultivated vineyards across its vast territories. Today, the Lazio region, in which Rome is situated, continues to produce excellent wines, many of which are enjoyed in the city's enotecas (wine bars) and trattorias. Frascati, a crisp white wine, is among the most celebrated local varieties and is often referred to as "the wine of Rome." This light, refreshing wine comes from the idyllic hills of the Castelli Romani, just outside the city, where vineyards have thrived for centuries. Pairing perfectly with Roman cuisine, a chilled glass of Frascati is the ideal companion for a plate of fresh artichokes or a simple seafood dish. Its bright acidity and citrus notes make it a go-to choice for locals seeking a taste of tradition.

For red wine enthusiasts, Cesanese del Piglio is Lazio's pride—a full-bodied red with a deep ruby hue and flavors of ripe cherries, blackberries, and a hint of spice. This wine, often described as rustic yet elegant, has been gaining recognition beyond the region for its complexity and versatility. It pairs beautifully with classic Roman dishes like coda alla vaccinara (braised oxtail) or saltimbocca alla Romana, enhancing the hearty flavors of these meals with its rich profile. Cesanese is often enjoyed during cooler months, providing warmth and depth that mirror the city's ancient soul.

No Roman wine experience would be complete without a visit to an enoteca, where the city's love affair with wine is on full display. Enotecas, ranging from cozy neighborhood spots to more refined establishments, serve as the perfect place to explore the diversity of Italian wines. Cul de Sac, located near Piazza Navona, is one of the city's most beloved wine bars, offering an extensive menu that spans the entire Italian peninsula. With knowledgeable staff eager to guide you, you can sample wines from Lazio, Tuscany, Piedmont, Sicily, and beyond, pairing them with a selection of cheeses, cured meats, and other small plates. The atmosphere is warm and unpretentious, making it an ideal spot for both seasoned oenophiles and curious newcomers.

Beyond the enotecas, wine also plays a prominent role in the Roman aperitivo tradition, a cherished prelude to dinner where the focus is on sipping and snacking. Aperitivo is not simply a meal or a drink; it is a moment of transition, a pause in the day to relax and socialize before the evening begins. Typically enjoyed between 6:00 and 8:00 PM, aperitivo is a time when Romans gather in bars and piazzas to share a drink and small bites, reflecting the Italian ideal of dolce far niente—the sweetness of doing nothing. The drinks themselves can range from a glass of wine to more complex cocktails, but the emphasis is always on balance and moderation.

The Aperol Spritz is perhaps the most iconic aperitivo drink in Rome, with its vibrant orange hue and effervescent character. Made from Aperol, prosecco, and a splash of soda, this refreshing cocktail is equal parts bitter and sweet, making it the perfect accompaniment to salty snacks like olives, chips, or bruschetta. Its low alcohol content ensures that it whets the appetite without overwhelming the palate, setting the stage for the meal to come. Many bars in Rome serve Aperol Spritzes with a small plate of complimentary snacks, making it an affordable and enjoyable way to ease into the evening.

For those who prefer something with a bit more complexity, the Negroni is a classic choice. This bold cocktail, made from equal parts gin, Campari, and sweet vermouth, embodies the spirit of Italian aperitivo culture with its strong, bittersweet flavor profile. Often served with a twist of orange peel, the Negroni is a drink for those who appreciate bold flavors and a touch of sophistication. Its cousin, the Negroni Sbagliato, replaces gin with sparkling wine, resulting in a lighter, fizzier alternative that is equally satisfying.

While cocktails are a popular choice, many Romans opt for a simple glass of wine during aperitivo, often choosing lighter, easy-drinking varieties that pair well with the small plates offered at bars. White wines like Vermentino or Falanghina and reds like Montepulciano d'Abruzzo are common choices, providing a taste of Italy's diverse wine regions in an unpretentious setting. These wines, though often humble in price, are carefully selected to enhance the aperitivo experience, proving that quality need not come with a hefty price tag.

The food served during aperitivo is just as important as the drinks, and Roman bars take pride in offering a tempting array of snacks that elevate the experience. Traditional offerings include supplì (fried rice balls filled with mozzarella), bruschetta topped with tomatoes and basil, and small plates of cured meats and cheeses. Some places, like Freni e Frizioni in Trastevere, go above and beyond, offering a full buffet of creative dishes that cater to a variety of tastes and dietary preferences. This approach transforms aperitivo into a more substantial affair, allowing patrons to linger over their drinks while sampling a wide range of flavors.

One of the joys of aperitivo in Rome is the variety of settings in which it can be enjoyed. From trendy rooftop bars with panoramic views of the city to cozy, dimly lit establishments tucked away in cobblestoned alleys, there is an aperitivo spot to suit every mood and occasion. The terrazza at Hotel Raphael, located near Piazza Navona, offers a stunning backdrop of Roman rooftops and domes, making it an ideal choice for a special evening. On the other hand, Bar del Fico, with its bohemian vibe and lively outdoor seating area, is perfect for a casual gathering with friends.

The beauty of Roman wine and aperitivo culture lies in its accessibility and inclusivity. It is not reserved for special occasions or the wealthy; it is a daily ritual that anyone can partake in, from the business professional unwinding after work to the group of friends celebrating a milestone. It is a culture that values the simple pleasures of life—good food, good drink, and good company—reminding us that joy can be found in the smallest of moments.

To drink like a Roman is to embrace this ethos, to slow down and savor the experience. It is about choosing quality over quantity, taking the time to appreciate the craft behind each glass of wine or cocktail, and recognizing the importance of the people and places that make these moments special. Whether you are sipping a glass of Frascati at a bustling enoteca or enjoying an Aperol Spritz as the sun sets over the Tiber, you are participating in a tradition that has been perfected over centuries. It is a tradition that speaks to the heart of Rome itself, a city that knows how to celebrate life in all its flavors.

Food Markets to Explore: Campo de' Fiori, Testaccio, and More

Rome's food markets are vibrant, sensory-rich hubs that offer more than just groceries; they are windows into the city's soul, showcasing its culinary traditions, seasonal produce, and the rhythm of daily life. Exploring these markets is not merely about shopping—it's an immersion into the sights, sounds, and flavors of Rome. From bustling open-air squares to modern covered markets, these spaces are where locals and visitors alike can discover the freshest ingredients, artisanal products, and the essence of Roman culture. Whether you're hunting for the perfect pecorino cheese, sampling sun-ripened tomatoes, or simply watching the lively exchanges between vendors and customers, Rome's food markets are a feast for the senses.

Campo de' Fiori is perhaps the most iconic market in the city, its name and presence steeped in history. Located in a lively square in the heart of Rome, the market has been a gathering place for centuries, though its purpose has evolved over time. Once a site for public executions, it is now a bustling open-air market where colorful stalls brim with fresh produce, flowers, spices, and local delicacies. Early morning is the best time to visit, when the vendors are setting up, the produce is at its freshest, and the square is bathed in soft Roman sunlight. The air is filled with the aroma of ripe fruits, herbs, and freshly baked bread, mingled with the chatter of vendors calling out their wares.

One of the highlights of Campo de' Fiori is its unparalleled selection of seasonal fruits and vegetables. Italian cuisine is firmly rooted in the seasons, and this market is a testament to that philosophy. In spring, you'll find piles of artichokes—both the Roman-style carciofi and the spikier varieties—ready to be transformed into carciofi alla Romana or carciofi alla giudia. Summer brings an explosion of color with juicy peaches, fragrant melons, and vibrant tomatoes that are perfect for a simple caprese salad. Autumn is the season for porcini mushrooms, chestnuts, and deep orange pumpkins, while winter offers hearty greens like kale and chicory. Vendors often encourage you to taste their produce, slicing open a peach or tomato to reveal its sweet, juicy interior—a gesture that reflects the pride they take in their offerings.

Beyond produce, Campo de' Fiori is also a treasure trove of Roman staples and specialties. Stalls sell everything from dried pasta and olive oils to regional cheeses and cured meats. One vendor may offer wedges of Pecorino Romano, its salty tang a perfect match for a plate of cacio e pepe, while another displays trays of guanciale, the cured pork jowl essential for making carbonara or amatriciana. You'll also find jars of artichokes preserved in olive oil, vibrant green pesto, and an array of spices that reflect Rome's culinary heritage. For those with a sweet tooth, stalls selling candied fruits, biscotti, and torrone (nougat) provide the perfect indulgence.

While Campo de' Fiori is undeniably popular with tourists, its energy and authenticity remain intact. The vendors, many of whom have been selling here for generations, are eager to share their knowledge and may even offer cooking tips or recipes if you show genuine interest. Nearby, the surrounding streets are home to bakeries, butchers, and wine shops that complement the market experience, making Campo de' Fiori a one-stop destination for anyone looking to delve into Roman gastronomy.

For a more authentic, less touristy experience, the Testaccio market is a must-visit. Situated in the historic Testaccio neighborhood, which has long been considered the heart of Roman cuisine, this modern covered market combines tradition with innovation. Unlike the open-air charm of Campo de' Fiori, Testaccio's market is housed in a sleek, well-organized structure that offers both convenience and a sense of community. It is a place where locals do their daily shopping, and the atmosphere is lively yet unpretentious.

At the heart of the Testaccio market is its dedication to quality and tradition. Vendors here take their craft seriously, whether they are butchers selling cuts of meat for traditional Roman dishes, fishmongers displaying the freshest catches from the Mediterranean, or produce sellers offering an array of vibrant fruits and vegetables. One standout is Mordi e Vai, a stall famous for its panini stuffed with classic Roman fillings like allesso di bollito (slow-cooked beef) or tripe in tomato sauce. These sandwiches are a delicious way to sample traditional flavors in a casual, accessible format.

Another gem within the Testaccio market is Casa Manco, a pizzeria that redefines the concept of pizza al taglio (pizza by the slice). Their dough, fermented for 72 hours, is light and airy, and the toppings range from classic margherita to inventive combinations like figs with gorgonzola and walnuts. For dessert, head to Dess'Art for a selection of freshly baked pastries, or stop by one of the stalls selling artisanal gelato. The market also boasts several vendors specializing in organic and locally sourced products, reflecting the growing interest in sustainability and health-conscious eating.

Testaccio's culinary significance extends beyond its market. The neighborhood itself is a living testament to Rome's food history, once serving as the city's slaughterhouse district and giving rise to many of its most iconic dishes, such as coda alla vaccinara and pajata. Exploring the market in Testaccio offers a deeper understanding of the ingredients and traditions that define Roman cuisine, as well as a chance to interact with the people who keep these traditions alive.

Campo de' Fiori and Testaccio may be the most well-known markets, but Rome has many others waiting to be discovered. Mercato Trionfale, located near the Vatican, is one of the largest and most comprehensive markets in the city. With over 270 stalls, it offers an impressive variety of products, from fresh seafood and meats to cheeses, wines, and international ingredients. The market's sheer scale can feel overwhelming, but it also ensures that you'll find everything you need, whether you're planning a picnic or seeking out hard-to-find items.

For a more bohemian vibe, the San Cosimato market in Trastevere is a charming option. Smaller and more intimate than some of the city's other markets, San Cosimato exudes a neighborhood feel, with vendors greeting regular customers by name. The produce is fresh and reasonably priced, and the market also features stalls selling flowers, baked goods, and household items. Its location in the heart of Trastevere makes it a convenient stop while exploring the area's narrow streets and hidden piazzas.

Piazza Vittorio's Nuovo Mercato Esquilino offers a completely different experience, reflecting the multicultural diversity of modern Rome. This indoor market is a melting pot of flavors, with stalls selling ingredients from all over the world, including spices from India, teas from China, and exotic fruits from South America. It's a fantastic place to find ingredients that aren't typically associated with Italian cuisine, making it a favorite among adventurous cooks and those seeking to expand their culinary horizons.

Exploring Rome's food markets is not just about shopping for ingredients—it's about connecting with the city's traditions, its people, and its vibrant energy. Each market has its own personality, shaped by its location, vendors, and clientele. Whether you're wandering through the historic charm of Campo de' Fiori, delving into the culinary heritage of Testaccio, or uncovering hidden gems in Trionfale or Esquilino, these markets offer a glimpse into the heart of Roman life. They remind us that food is more than sustenance; it is culture, community, and a celebration of the seasons. For anyone seeking to understand Rome, its food markets are the perfect place to start.

Vegetarian and Vegan Options in a Meat-Heavy City

Rome, a city renowned for its rich culinary heritage, is often associated with hearty, meat-centric dishes like carbonara, amatriciana, and coda alla vaccinara. However, for vegetarians and vegans, navigating this traditionally meat-heavy cuisine doesn't mean sacrificing flavor or authenticity. The Eternal City offers an abundance of plant-based options, rooted in its history of cucina povera—"poor kitchen"—a simple yet ingenious style of cooking that highlights seasonal vegetables, legumes, and grains. With a little guidance, vegetarians and vegans can uncover a bounty of satisfying dishes and dedicated eateries that prove Rome's food scene is far more versatile than it might initially appear.

The foundation of vegetarian-friendly Roman cuisine lies in the city's love affair with vegetables. Artichokes, zucchini, eggplants, tomatoes, chicory, and puntarelle (a type of curly chicory) are staples of the Roman diet, celebrated in dishes that showcase their natural flavors. Carciofi alla Romana, or Roman-style artichokes, is a prime example. Artichokes are stuffed with a mixture of garlic and fresh herbs like parsley and mint before being gently braised in olive oil and white wine until tender. This dish, which is naturally vegan, is a seasonal favorite during the spring when artichokes are at their peak. Similarly, carciofi alla giudia, a specialty of Rome's Jewish Ghetto, involves deep-frying whole artichokes until their leaves turn golden and crispy, creating a dish that is as visually stunning as it is delicious.

Zucchini flowers, or fiori di zucca, are another vegetable-based delight. These delicate blossoms are typically stuffed with ricotta cheese and fried to perfection. While the traditional version contains cheese, many restaurants and trattorias offer variations that cater to vegans by using plant-based fillings or no filling at all. The crunch of the batter combined with the subtle sweetness of the zucchini flower makes this dish a must-try. Another vegetable staple is puntarelle, often served as a salad with a tangy anchovy dressing. For vegans, some places replace the anchovy with a citrusy vinaigrette, allowing the bitter, crisp greens to shine.

Pasta, a cornerstone of Roman cuisine, offers a treasure trove of vegetarian options. While dishes like carbonara and amatriciana are off the table for those avoiding meat, classics such as cacio e pepe and pasta alla gricia can easily be adapted. Cacio e pepe, a deceptively simple dish made with Pecorino Romano cheese and black pepper, is naturally vegetarian and highlights the elegance of minimal ingredients. For vegans, some restaurants now offer plant-based versions using cashew cream or nutritional yeast to replicate the creamy texture and salty bite of the cheese.

Aglio e olio, a garlic and olive oil-based pasta dish, is another naturally vegan option. Enhanced with a sprinkle of red pepper flakes for heat, this dish is a testament to the cucina povera tradition of creating something extraordinary out of pantry staples. Another classic pasta offering is pasta e ceci, a comforting blend of pasta and chickpeas cooked in a rich tomato and rosemary-infused broth. This dish, which harks back to Rome's rustic roots, is both filling and flavorful, appealing to vegetarians and vegans alike.

For those seeking plant-based pizza, Rome does not disappoint. Roman-style pizza, characterized by its thin, crispy crust, lends itself beautifully to vegetable toppings. Pizza bianca, a simple yet iconic Roman creation, is topped with olive oil, sea salt, and rosemary, making it naturally vegan and addictively delicious. Pizzerias across the city also offer a range of vegetarian and vegan options, from classic margherita to pizzas loaded with grilled vegetables, mushrooms, or even truffle oil for a touch of indulgence. Many modern pizzerias now provide vegan cheese alternatives, allowing for even greater customization.

Rome's food markets are an essential stop for any vegetarian or vegan looking to explore the city's culinary offerings. Campo de' Fiori, Testaccio Market, and Trionfale Market are brimming with fresh, seasonal produce, legumes, nuts, and grains that can be transformed into satisfying meals. Many vendors sell ready-to-eat options like roasted vegetables, marinated olives, or freshly baked bread, making these markets ideal for a quick yet delicious lunch. Exploring these markets also provides insight into the diversity and quality of ingredients that form the backbone of Roman cuisine.

Dedicated vegetarian and vegan eateries are on the rise in Rome, catering to locals and tourists who prefer plant-based dining. Ops!, located in the Prati district, is a popular vegan restaurant offering a pay-by-weight buffet that features an impressive array of salads, grains, roasted vegetables, and plant-based proteins. The vibrant dishes change daily, ensuring there's always something new to try. Another standout is Rifugio Romano, a family-run restaurant that offers both traditional Roman dishes and vegan adaptations. Their vegan carbonara, made with tofu and soy cream, and their plant-based tiramisu are particularly beloved by diners.

For a more casual experience, Universo Vegano, a chain of vegan fast-food restaurants, serves up burgers, wraps, and bowls made entirely from plant-based ingredients. The portions are generous, and the flavors are bold, making it a great option for those on the go. Similarly, Flower Burger, another vegan burger chain, offers colorful, Instagram-worthy burgers with unique flavors and house-made sauces. These spots are perfect for a quick meal without compromising on taste or quality.

Desserts, often a challenge for vegans in traditional cuisine, are no exception in Rome. Many gelaterias now offer dairy-free gelato made from almond, soy, or oat milk, ensuring that everyone can indulge in this quintessential Italian treat. Gelateria del Teatro and Fatamorgana are two standout options, offering a wide range of vegan flavors, from dark chocolate to fruit sorbets bursting with natural sweetness. Meanwhile, bakeries like Grezzo Raw Chocolate specialize in vegan and raw desserts, including decadent pastries, truffles, and even vegan cannoli.

Navigating Roman dining as a vegetarian or vegan also means understanding the cultural nuances of restaurant menus. While many dishes are inherently plant-based, it's always a good idea to confirm with your server, as some recipes may include hidden animal products like lard or chicken broth. Romans are generally accommodating and take pride in their hospitality, so don't hesitate to ask for modifications or recommendations. Even in traditional trattorias, chefs are often willing to prepare a simple plate of pasta with olive oil, garlic, and seasonal vegetables upon request.

Rome's drinking culture also caters to plant-based preferences, with plenty of options for vegan wine and aperitivo. Many Italian wines are naturally vegan, as traditional winemaking processes rely on minimal intervention. Enotecas (wine bars) across the city often showcase organic and biodynamic wines, providing an excellent opportunity to sample vegan-friendly options. Aperitivo, the pre-dinner ritual of drinks and small bites, frequently includes vegetarian snacks like bruschetta with tomatoes, olives, and roasted peppers. Some modern bars now offer plant-based spreads, ensuring that vegans can fully enjoy this cherished Roman tradition.

Rome's evolving food scene reflects a growing awareness of vegetarian and vegan diets, blending traditional flavors with innovative approaches to plant-based cooking. Whether you're savoring a plate of carciofi alla Romana, indulging in vegan gelato, or exploring the city's vibrant food markets, it's clear that Rome has embraced the diversity of culinary preferences without losing its authentic spirit. For vegetarians and vegans, the Eternal City offers not only sustenance but also a deeper connection to its culture, proving that plant-based dining can be as rich and rewarding as any Roman feast.

Dining Etiquette in Rome: Tips for Eating Out

Dining in Rome is not just about the food on your plate; it's an experience steeped in tradition, culture, and unspoken rules. For first-time visitors, understanding the nuances of Roman dining etiquette can elevate your meals from enjoyable to truly memorable. Italians take their meals seriously, viewing them as a time to relax, connect, and celebrate the art of good food. While Roman restaurants offer a relaxed atmosphere, there are customs and practices that might surprise the uninitiated. Knowing how to navigate these can help you blend in with the locals and show your appreciation for their way of life.

One of the first things to understand is how meal times work in Rome. Romans are creatures of habit, and their dining schedule reflects this. Lunch, or "pranzo," is typically eaten between 1:00 PM and 3:00 PM, while dinner, or "cena," starts late by many international standards, usually around 8:00 PM or later. If you arrive at a restaurant at 6:30 PM expecting dinner, you may find the place empty or even closed as the staff prepares for the evening rush. Adjusting to Roman dining hours is important if you want to avoid disappointment. For those who can't wait until dinner, aperitivo—a pre-dinner ritual involving drinks and small snacks—is an excellent way to bridge the gap.

When it comes to choosing a restaurant, authenticity is key. Romans take pride in their local trattorias (casual, family-run eateries) and osterias (informal taverns) that serve traditional dishes. Avoid places with overly touristy menus displaying pictures of food or offering dishes that don't belong to Roman cuisine, such as spaghetti bolognese or pineapple pizza. A good rule of thumb is to watch where the locals go; a bustling trattoria filled with Italians chatting over plates of cacio e pepe or amatriciana is a sure sign of quality. Reservations are often recommended, especially for dinner, as many popular establishments can fill up quickly. A quick phone call or even stopping by earlier in the day to reserve a table can save you from a long wait or being turned away.

Upon arriving at the restaurant, don't expect to be seated immediately without a reservation. Hosts at Roman eateries might ask for your name if you've booked in advance or let you know how long the wait will be. Once seated, you'll notice that service in Rome is less hurried than it might be in other countries. Meals are meant to be enjoyed leisurely, so don't expect your server to rush over with menus or push you to order quickly. Take your time, settle in, and soak up the atmosphere. Unlike in some cultures, calling a server over with a wave or shout is considered rude. Instead, make gentle eye contact or raise your hand slightly to signal that you're ready.

The menu itself may require some decoding for those unfamiliar with the structure of Italian dining. Traditional meals are divided into several courses: antipasti (starters), primi (first courses, usually pasta or risotto), secondi (main courses, typically meat or fish), contorni (side dishes like vegetables or salads), and dolci (desserts). While it's customary for Italians to order multiple courses, it's perfectly acceptable to choose fewer dishes if you prefer. However, keep in mind that sides are often ordered separately from main courses, so if you want vegetables or potatoes with your secondo, you'll need to ask for them. Bread, or "pane," is usually brought to the table automatically, but it's not complimentary; a small charge called "coperto" will appear on your bill to cover bread and table service. It's worth noting that bread in Rome is often quite plain and intended to complement the meal rather than serve as an appetizer.

When it comes to ordering, Italians value dishes made with fresh, seasonal ingredients. Don't hesitate to ask your server for recommendations or inquire about daily specials, known as "piatti del giorno." This is often the best way to experience dishes that highlight the flavors of the season. Additionally,

Roman cuisine is deeply rooted in tradition, so sticking to local specialties will likely result in a more satisfying meal. Ordering a dish like spaghetti carbonara, saltimbocca alla Romana, or carciofi alla giudia shows an appreciation for the city's culinary heritage.

Wine is an integral part of dining in Rome, and selecting the right bottle or glass can enhance your meal. Most restaurants offer a house wine, or "vino della casa," which is often of excellent quality and reasonably priced. If you'd like something more specific, consult the wine list or ask your server for suggestions. In Italy, wine is seen as an accompaniment to food rather than a standalone drink, so it's rare to see locals sipping wine without a meal. Similarly, water is always served alongside wine, and you'll be asked if you prefer "acqua naturale" (still water) or "acqua frizzante" (sparkling water). Tap water is not typically served in restaurants, so bottled water is the standard.

As you enjoy your meal, you'll notice that Romans place a strong emphasis on table manners. Eating is a communal activity, and good etiquette ensures that everyone at the table has a pleasant experience. For instance, cutting spaghetti with a knife or using a spoon to twirl it is considered a faux pas; instead, use your fork to roll the pasta against the side of your plate. Sharing dishes is common, especially with antipasti or desserts, but it's polite to ask before diving into someone else's plate. If you're eating pizza, keep in mind that it's typically served as an individual portion rather than a shared dish. Romans often use a knife and fork to eat their pizza, especially in sit-down restaurants, although no one will judge you for picking up a slice with your hands in a more casual setting.

Tipping in Rome is another area where visitors often have questions. Unlike in some countries, tipping is not obligatory in Italy, as service charges are usually included in the bill. However, if you've received exceptional service, leaving a small tip—rounding up the bill or leaving a few euros—is appreciated but not expected. Be aware that credit card slips in Italy often don't have a line for adding a tip, so it's best to leave cash if you choose to tip.

Once you've finished your meal, don't expect the check, or "il conto," to arrive automatically. In Italy, it's considered impolite to rush diners, so you'll need to ask your server when you're ready to pay. Simply say, "Il conto, per favore," and your server will bring it to you. Take your time settling the bill; there's no pressure to vacate your table quickly, as Italians often linger over an espresso or digestivo (a post-meal liqueur) after their meal.

Dining out in Rome is as much about the experience as it is about the food. By embracing the city's customs and traditions, you'll not only enjoy better meals but also gain a deeper appreciation for Roman culture. Whether you're savoring a plate of pasta in a bustling trattoria or sharing stories over an aperitivo with friends, the act of eating in Rome is a celebration of life's simple pleasures—and the more you immerse yourself in this ritual, the more rewarding your culinary journey will be.

CHAPTER 6: ROME BY NIGHT

Evening Strolls: The Magic of Rome's Illuminated Landmarks

As the sun dips below the horizon and the warm hues of twilight give way to the cool blue of night, Rome undergoes a transformation. The Eternal City, renowned for its historical grandeur by day, unveils a softer, more enchanting side under the glow of its evening lights. Illuminated landmarks cast their reflections on cobblestone streets, fountains glisten under the moonlight, and the hum of life continues in a quieter, more romantic rhythm. To truly understand Rome, one must experience it after dark, when its monuments and piazzas exude a magic that feels almost otherworldly. Evening strolls through Rome are not just a way to explore the city, but an invitation to immerse yourself in its timeless beauty, discovering something new even in the most familiar places.

The Colosseum, one of the most iconic symbols of Rome, takes on an entirely different character at night. Bathed in golden light, its ancient arches and walls stand in stark contrast to the dark sky, evoking its storied past with a haunting beauty. Walking along Via dei Fori Imperiali toward the Colosseum in the evening, you can almost hear the echoes of history—the roar of crowds, the clash of gladiators, and the whispers of emperors who once ruled from their thrones. The traffic that normally surrounds this monument during the day slows in the evening, allowing you to take in its majesty without distraction. The stillness of the night amplifies its grandeur, and standing before it, you may feel the weight of centuries pressing down in the most awe-inspiring way.

Not far from the Colosseum lies the Roman Forum, a collection of ruins that served as the political and social heart of ancient Rome. While the Forum is open for exploration during the day, its evening ambiance is unparalleled. The softly lit columns, arches, and temples create an almost ethereal atmosphere, as if the city's ancient spirits have awakened to reclaim their space. Gazing at the illuminated ruins from the Capitoline Hill offers a breathtaking perspective, with the twinkling lights of modern Rome in the distance providing a poignant reminder of the city's enduring legacy. The contrast between the ruins and the bustling city feels like a bridge between two worlds, where past and present coexist harmoniously.

A short walk away, Piazza Venezia buzzes with energy even after the sun sets. Dominating the square is the Vittorio Emanuele II Monument, also known as the Altar of the Fatherland, an imposing structure that gleams brilliantly under its nighttime illumination. While some may find its size overwhelming during the day, the soft lighting at night lends it a certain elegance. Climbing the steps to the terrace offers a panoramic view of the city's rooftops, their terracotta tiles glowing faintly in the light of the streetlamps below. From this vantage point, the city feels alive yet peaceful, a sprawling maze of history and humanity united under the Roman sky.

Wandering through the narrow streets toward Piazza Navona, the charm of Rome's evening strolls becomes even more apparent. The piazza, which is lively during the day, transforms into a serene yet vibrant gathering place at night. Street performers, musicians, and artists share the space with couples and families, all basking in the soft glow of the baroque fountains. Bernini's Fountain of the Four Rivers, illuminated and shimmering, becomes the centerpiece of the square, its sculpted figures casting dramatic shadows that seem to move with the flicker of the lights. The surrounding cafés and trattorias hum with quiet laughter and the clinking of glasses, offering the perfect spot to pause with a glass of wine and watch the world go by.

The nearby Pantheon, a marvel of ancient engineering, is equally captivating under the cover of night. Unlike its daytime crowds, the evening draws fewer visitors, allowing for a more intimate encounter with this architectural masterpiece. Standing before its massive columns, you can appreciate the scale and precision of its construction without the distractions of the bustling piazza. The floodlights accentuate the details of its façade, highlighting the weathered textures of its stone and the inscriptions that have withstood the test of time. The Pantheon's dome, visible against the night sky, serves as a reminder of Rome's enduring genius, a beacon that has inspired artists, architects, and dreamers for centuries.

A short walk south brings you to Campo de' Fiori, a lively square that embodies Rome's vibrant nightlife. During the day, this piazza hosts a bustling market filled with vendors selling fresh produce, flowers, and spices, but at night, it transforms into a hub of social activity. The statue of Giordano Bruno, standing solemnly in the center, watches over the mingling crowds as they gather at outdoor tables and bars. The square's energy is infectious, with the laughter of friends and the clinking of glasses filling the air. For those seeking a more casual evening, Campo de' Fiori offers an array of options, from sipping a spritz to enjoying a late-night gelato as you soak in the lively atmosphere.

Crossing the Tiber River via the illuminated Ponte Sisto leads you to Trastevere, one of Rome's most charming neighborhoods. Known for its bohemian spirit and winding cobblestone streets, Trastevere truly comes alive at night. The warm glow of streetlamps reflects off the ivy-covered buildings, and the aroma of freshly baked pizza and simmering sauces wafts through the air. Wandering through its labyrinthine alleys feels like stepping into a timeless village, where every corner reveals a new delight. Piazza Santa Maria, with its namesake basilica, serves as the heart of Trastevere's nightlife, its fountain and church façade glowing softly in the evening light. The neighborhood's trattorias and wine bars invite you to linger, savoring the flavors and stories that make this corner of Rome so special.

For a quieter, more reflective evening stroll, the Janiculum Hill offers a tranquil escape from the city's bustling streets. This vantage point, less frequented by tourists, provides some of the most spectacular views of Rome. As the city lights stretch out before you, the dome of St. Peter's Basilica rises majestically, illuminated like a crown jewel against the dark backdrop. The walk up the hill, though steep, is rewarded with a sense of serenity and the opportunity to see Rome from a different perspective. The Gianicolo Lighthouse, a lesser-known landmark, adds to the charm with its colorful beams of light that sweep across the skyline.

The Spanish Steps, another iconic Roman landmark, are particularly enchanting at night. The crowds that swarm the steps during the day thin out as evening falls, leaving a quieter space to appreciate their beauty. The Trinità dei Monti church at the top of the steps glows softly, while the Fontana della Barcaccia at the base sparkles in the moonlight. Sitting on the steps, you can watch as the city slows down, with the occasional street performer adding a touch of whimsy to the scene.

No evening stroll in Rome would be complete without a visit to the Trevi Fountain. This baroque masterpiece, already stunning during the day, becomes utterly magical at night. The fountain's cascading waters, illuminated by soft lights, seem to dance as they catch the glow. Tossing a coin into the fountain, a tradition said to ensure your return to Rome, feels even more intimate under the cover of darkness. The sound of the water, combined with the hushed whispers of visitors, creates an almost sacred atmosphere, making it a fitting end to any evening exploration.

Rome's illuminated landmarks are more than just beautiful sights; they are living stories, each one offering a glimpse into the city's soul. As you wander through its streets, the interplay of light and shadow reveals details that go unnoticed during the day, breathing new life into even the most familiar monuments. These evening strolls are a reminder that Rome is a city meant to be experienced not just with your eyes, but with your heart. Every step, every glance, and every moment spent under its glowing lights is an invitation to fall in love with the Eternal City all over again.

Nightlife Hotspots: Bars, Clubs, and Live Music

Rome, a city celebrated for its timeless history and architectural splendor, reveals a different side as the sun sets and its streets come alive with the hum of nightlife. The Eternal City's nocturnal offerings are as diverse as its cultural heritage. From sophisticated wine bars tucked into cobblestone alleys to lively clubs where DJs spin until dawn, and intimate venues hosting live music performances, Rome's nightlife caters to every taste and mood. Whether you're seeking a quiet drink with friends, a chance to dance the night away, or a soulful concert in a historic setting, the city provides a wealth of opportunities to explore after dark.

The heart of Rome's nightlife often begins in its piazzas, which transform into vibrant social hubs as evening falls. Campo de' Fiori, known for its bustling market during the day, becomes a lively gathering place at night. The square is lined with bars and pubs catering to both locals and tourists, offering a laid-back atmosphere perfect for starting your evening. One of the most popular spots is Drunken Ship, a lively pub that draws a younger crowd with its affordable drinks and energetic vibe. Across the square, you'll find more refined establishments like Magnolia, where you can sip on expertly crafted cocktails while soaking in the lively buzz of the piazza. The beauty of Campo de' Fiori lies in its accessibility—whether you're seeking a casual beer or a sophisticated drink, the options are abundant.

For those who prefer a more elegant start to their evening, Piazza Navona offers a selection of upscale cocktail bars with stunning views of its fountains and baroque architecture. Bar del Fico, just a few steps away from the piazza, is a favorite haunt among locals. Its bohemian-chic interior and outdoor seating under twinkling lights make it an inviting spot for an aperitivo or a late-night drink. The bar's signature cocktails, often featuring Italian liqueurs like limoncello or amaro, are a testament to the creativity and craftsmanship of Rome's mixologists. As you sip your drink and watch the lively chatter unfold around you, it's easy to see why Romans treasure their evenings as a time for connection and relaxation.

Trastevere, on the other side of the Tiber River, is a neighborhood that radiates charm and energy, particularly after dark. Its narrow streets and ivy-clad buildings lead to hidden gems that embody the spirit of Roman nightlife. Freni e Frizioni, housed in a former mechanic's garage, is a trendy bar known for its inventive cocktails and vegan aperitivo buffet. The outdoor terrace overlooking Piazza Trilussa is always bustling, making it an ideal spot for people-watching. Nearby, La Punta Expendio de Agave offers a completely different experience, specializing in tequila and mezcal-based cocktails that transport you to Mexico while still feeling uniquely Roman. Trastevere's eclectic mix of bars ensures that there's always something new to discover, no matter how many times you visit.

For a more contemporary take on Roman nightlife, the Testaccio district is a must-visit. Once the city's slaughterhouse district, Testaccio has reinvented itself as a hub for music and dancing. At the heart of this transformation is Via di Monte Testaccio, a street lined with clubs and bars built into ancient caves formed from discarded amphorae. One of the most iconic venues is Akab, a club that has been a fixture of Rome's nightlife scene for decades. With its mix of live music, DJ sets, and themed nights, Akab attracts a diverse crowd looking to dance and celebrate until the early hours.

Another standout is Goa Club, renowned for its cutting-edge electronic music and international DJs. The club's sleek, industrial design and state-of-the-art sound system create an immersive experience that keeps partygoers coming back.

If live music is more your scene, Rome offers an array of venues showcasing everything from jazz and blues to indie rock and classical performances. Alexanderplatz, one of the oldest jazz clubs in the city, is a beloved institution for its intimate atmosphere and impressive lineup of local and international artists. Tucked away near the Vatican, this cozy basement venue invites you to lose yourself in the smooth melodies of a saxophone or the soulful vocals of a jazz singer. For a more contemporary vibe, Monk Club in the Tiburtina district hosts an eclectic mix of live music and cultural events. Its outdoor space, complete with string lights and picnic tables, is perfect for summer evenings, while the indoor stage provides a dynamic setting for concerts year-round.

Rome's larger music venues also play a significant role in its nightlife. Auditorium Parco della Musica, designed by renowned architect Renzo Piano, is a cultural landmark that hosts concerts spanning every genre imaginable. From classical symphonies to rock legends, the auditorium's calendar is filled with performances that attract both locals and visitors. During the summer, the venue's outdoor amphitheater comes alive with open-air concerts that allow you to enjoy world-class music under the stars. Similarly, Teatro dell'Opera di Roma offers an unforgettable experience for fans of opera and ballet. The opulent interior and exceptional acoustics make every performance feel like a special occasion, providing a glimpse into Rome's rich artistic heritage.

For those who crave a rooftop view to accompany their evening drink, Rome's skyline offers no shortage of options. The city's rooftop bars provide a unique perspective, with panoramic views of ancient ruins and modern landmarks alike. Terrazza Borromini, located atop Palazzo Pamphilj near Piazza Navona, combines stunning vistas with expertly crafted cocktails. Watching the sun set over the rooftops of Rome while sipping on a refreshing Negroni is an experience that captures the essence of la dolce vita. Another standout is Cielo Terrace at the Hotel de la Ville, where the elegant ambiance and sweeping views of the Spanish Steps create a magical setting for an unforgettable evening.

For a more alternative nightlife experience, the San Lorenzo district is a vibrant enclave known for its youthful energy and artistic flair. Popular among students and creatives, San Lorenzo is home to dive bars, live music venues, and street art that reflect its bohemian spirit. Marmo, located in a former marble workshop, is a stylish bar with an outdoor patio that often hosts live music and cultural events. The laid-back atmosphere and innovative cocktails make it a favorite among locals looking to unwind. Nearby, Ex Dogana offers a sprawling industrial space that hosts everything from electronic music festivals to art exhibitions, blending culture and nightlife in a way that feels uniquely Roman.

As the night winds down, many Romans turn to late-night eateries for a final bite before heading home. Pizzerias like Ai Marmi in Trastevere stay open late, serving up thin, crispy Roman-style pizza to satisfy post-drink cravings. For something sweet, gelaterias like Fatamorgana or Gelateria del Teatro offer a wide selection of flavors that provide the perfect ending to a lively evening. The tradition of grabbing a late-night snack is just another way that Romans savor life, finding joy in every moment, whether it's the first sip of an aperitivo or the last bite of pizza before bed.

Rome's nightlife is a tapestry woven with history, culture, and modern innovation. Each neighborhood offers its own unique flavor, from the bohemian charm of Trastevere to the pulsating beats of Testaccio's clubs. Whether you're sipping a cocktail under the stars, dancing until dawn, or losing yourself in the melodies of a live performance, the city invites you to embrace its vibrant energy after dark. As the lights of Rome illuminate its streets and landmarks, the Eternal City comes alive in a way that is both timeless and electric, promising unforgettable nights for all who wander its paths.

Evening Dining: Late-Night Eats and Romantic Restaurants

Rome reveals its most intimate and indulgent side during the evening hours, when the city slows down and its culinary scene takes center stage. Dining in the Eternal City is not merely about satisfying hunger; it's a ritual, a celebration of flavors, and often an unhurried affair that stretches late into the night. Whether you're in search of a romantic restaurant to share a candlelit meal or a cozy spot for some authentic late-night eats, Rome promises a dining experience steeped in atmosphere and tradition. The city's restaurants, trattorias, and osterias come alive after sunset, illuminated by soft golden light, with tables spilling onto piazzas and narrow streets. This is when Rome feels most alive, yet most tranquil, where the joys of food and good company take precedence over the rush of daily life.

For those seeking an evening steeped in romance, few settings rival the charm of Rome's historic center. Around Piazza Navona, you'll find a wealth of dining options that pair exquisite meals with stunning views. One standout is Ristorante Aroma, located on the rooftop of Palazzo Manfredi. This Michelin-starred restaurant offers a breathtaking view of the Colosseum, its ancient arches glowing softly in the night. The menu is a refined take on Italian cuisine, featuring dishes like truffle risotto and perfectly seared sea bass. Dining here feels like stepping into a dream, with the backdrop of history creating an unforgettable atmosphere. The service is impeccable, attentive but never intrusive, ensuring you can focus on savoring each bite and the company of your loved one.

If you prefer a more intimate setting, the Trastevere neighborhood offers the perfect escape. Known for its ivy-covered façades and labyrinthine streets, Trastevere exudes romance at every turn. Spirito di Vino, a family-run restaurant housed in a 1,000-year-old building, combines history with culinary artistry. The wine cellar, once a granary in Roman times, is worth a visit in itself. The menu leans heavily on seasonal ingredients, with signature dishes like braised oxtail and fresh handmade pasta that evoke the essence of Roman cuisine. The dimly lit dining room, with its vaulted ceilings and rustic charm, sets the stage for an unforgettable evening.

For a more contemporary romantic experience, Roscioli Salumeria con Cucina blends the sophistication of fine dining with the warmth of a traditional deli. Located near Campo de' Fiori, this establishment is renowned for its exceptional charcuterie, cheeses, and pasta dishes. Their carbonara, made with the perfect balance of guanciale, pecorino, and egg, is widely regarded as one of the best in the city. While the space is cozy and unassuming, the quality of the food and the care with which it's prepared elevate it to one of Rome's most cherished dining destinations. Sharing a meal here feels intimate and personal, as if you've stumbled upon a local secret.

As the evening progresses, the city's late-night dining options come into their own, catering to night owls and those seeking a final indulgence before heading home. Supplì, Rome's beloved fried rice balls, are a staple of late-night snacking. At Supplizio, a small eatery near Piazza Navona, these golden orbs are elevated to an art form. Crisp on the outside and filled with rich, gooey mozzarella and ragù, they are the perfect handheld treat for wandering the cobblestone streets. Pair them with a glass of house wine, and you have a quintessential Roman experience that's both simple and deeply satisfying.

For a heartier late-night meal, look no further than Ai Marmi, a bustling pizzeria in Trastevere. Often called "The Morgue" for its long, marble-topped tables, this no-frills spot serves some of the best thin-crust pizza in the city. Open until the early hours, Ai Marmi attracts a mix of locals and tourists, all eager to enjoy classic Roman pizzas like margherita or capricciosa, fresh from the wood-fired oven. The atmosphere is lively and unpretentious, making it the perfect place to satisfy post-bar cravings or cap off a long day of exploring. Don't skip the fritti, a selection of fried starters like zucchini flowers and supplì that are just as beloved as the pizzas.

For those who prefer something sweet to end the evening, Rome's gelaterias remain a highlight. Gelateria del Teatro, located on a quiet street near Piazza Navona, offers artisanal gelato in flavors that showcase the best of Italy's ingredients. From Sicilian pistachio to Amalfi lemon and rosemary honey, each scoop is a testament to the artistry of gelato-making. Open late into the night, it's a favorite stop for couples strolling hand-in-hand or families soaking in the city's magic. The gelato here is rich and creamy, yet never overly sweet, allowing the purity of the flavors to shine through.

Beyond the historic center, the Testaccio district provides a glimpse into Rome's working-class roots and its unpretentious love of food. Known as the birthplace of cucina romana, Testaccio is home to many late-night eateries that honor traditional dishes. Flavio al Velavevodetto is a standout, offering hearty plates of cacio e pepe and amatriciana served in a warm, convivial setting. The restaurant's location, built into the side of Monte Testaccio, adds a touch of history to the meal, as the hill is made entirely of ancient pottery shards. Dining here feels like stepping into a bygone era, where simplicity and flavor take precedence over presentation.

Street food enthusiasts will find plenty to love in Rome's late-night scene. Food trucks and kiosks scattered throughout the city serve up everything from porchetta sandwiches to freshly fried calamari. One of the most iconic is Trapizzino, a hybrid of pizza and sandwich that has taken Rome by storm. Filled with classic Roman stews and sauces like chicken cacciatore or oxtail, these triangular pockets of dough are both portable and deeply satisfying. With locations across the city, Trapizzino is a go-to option for a quick bite that doesn't compromise on flavor.

For a truly unique late-night experience, the Jewish Ghetto offers an array of culinary delights steeped in history. Ba'Ghetto Milky, a kosher dairy restaurant, specializes in dishes like fried artichokes and ricotta-filled ravioli that reflect the neighborhood's rich cultural heritage. The quiet streets of the Ghetto, illuminated by soft streetlights, provide a serene backdrop for an evening meal. Dining here feels like a journey through time, where every dish tells a story of resilience and tradition.

The charm of Rome's evening dining lies in its diversity. Whether you're savoring a multi-course meal in a Michelin-starred restaurant, grabbing a slice of pizza from a bustling pizzeria, or indulging in gelato by the Tiber River, every experience feels uniquely Roman. The city's ability to balance elegance with authenticity, tradition with innovation, ensures that every meal is memorable. As the night deepens and the streets grow quieter, the flavors of Rome linger, a reminder of the city's enduring love affair with food and the joy it brings to those who embrace its culinary traditions.

Night Tours of Rome: A Unique Perspective After Dark

As the sun sets over Rome, the Eternal City takes on a new and mesmerizing identity. The golden hues of daylight give way to the soft glow of streetlamps, and the monuments that stand as testaments to centuries of history are bathed in an ethereal light. Rome at night offers a perspective that is entirely distinct from its daytime splendor, revealing secrets and stories that only emerge under the cover of darkness. Night tours in Rome provide an extraordinary opportunity to experience the city's rich heritage in a more intimate and atmospheric setting, where the noise of the day fades and the ancient streets seem to whisper their own tales.

The Colosseum, one of the city's most iconic landmarks, becomes particularly captivating after dark. Its massive structure, illuminated by golden lights, stands in dramatic contrast to the night sky. Opting for a night tour of the Colosseum allows you to explore this ancient amphitheater without the throngs of daytime crowds. Many guided tours offer access to areas that are typically closed during regular hours, such as the underground hypogeum where gladiators and wild animals once awaited their fate. Walking through these dimly lit corridors, it's hard not to feel transported to another era. The stories of epic battles and grand spectacles seem more tangible in the quiet of the night, the flickering lights casting shadows that bring the past to life. Standing in the arena, under the stars, offers a sense of awe that even the sunlit grandeur of the Colosseum cannot replicate.

A short distance away, the Roman Forum and Palatine Hill also reveal a different character during the evening hours. While these sites are often bustling with visitors during the day, night tours provide a serene and almost magical atmosphere. The ruins, softly illuminated, take on an almost otherworldly glow, and the absence of crowds allows for quiet reflection. Walking among the remnants of temples, basilicas, and arches, you can almost hear the echoes of ancient Rome's political and social life. Some tours incorporate multimedia elements, such as projections and audio guides, that recreate the Forum's former glory, providing a vivid sense of what this hub of Roman civilization might have looked and sounded like in its prime. The view from Palatine Hill, overlooking the illuminated Forum and the modern city beyond, is a breathtaking reminder of Rome's enduring legacy.

The Vatican Museums, a daytime favorite for visitors, offer an entirely different experience during their special evening openings. Exploring the museums at night not only allows you to avoid the daytime crowds but also creates an intimate and serene atmosphere that enhances the art and artifacts on display. The Sistine Chapel, in particular, feels even more sacred under the soft lighting of the evening. Standing beneath Michelangelo's masterpiece in near silence, you can fully appreciate the intricate details and the profound spirituality of the frescoes. Many night tours of the Vatican include exclusive access to areas that are typically closed to the public, such as the Bramante Staircase or the Niccoline Chapel, adding an extra layer of intrigue to the experience.

One of the most enchanting night tours in Rome is a walk through the city's piazzas and fountains. Piazza Navona, with its baroque fountains and lively atmosphere, becomes truly magical at night. The Fountain of the Four Rivers, designed by Bernini, glistens under the moonlight, its sculpted figures casting dramatic shadows. Nearby, the Pantheon, one of Rome's best-preserved ancient structures, takes on an almost mystical quality after dark. The floodlit façade highlights the grandeur of its columns and pediment, while the quieter piazza allows for uninterrupted admiration of this architectural marvel. Strolling through these iconic spaces at night, accompanied by a knowledgeable guide, provides fascinating insights into their history and significance, making the experience both educational and deeply moving.

No night tour of Rome would be complete without a visit to the Trevi Fountain. The fountain, already stunning during the day, becomes utterly mesmerizing at night. The cascading water, illuminated by soft lights, creates a mesmerizing play of movement and reflection. Tossing a coin into the fountain under the cover of darkness feels like participating in a ritual that is both timeless and deeply personal. Night tours that include the Trevi Fountain often delve into its history and the legends surrounding it, adding depth to the experience. The quieter evening hours also provide the perfect opportunity to take in the fountain's intricate details, from the sculpted figures to the carefully designed tiers of water.

For those seeking a more unconventional perspective, night tours of Rome's underground sites offer a thrilling and mysterious adventure. The Catacombs of Domitilla or San Sebastiano, located along the ancient Appian Way, provide a hauntingly beautiful glimpse into early Christian burial practices. Descending into these subterranean labyrinths with a guide, you'll learn about the art, inscriptions, and rituals of a time when Christianity was still emerging in the Roman Empire. The quiet and cool air of the catacombs, combined with the flickering light of lanterns, creates an atmosphere that is both eerie and awe-inspiring.

Equally compelling is a nighttime exploration of Castel Sant'Angelo. Originally built as a mausoleum for Emperor Hadrian, the structure has served many purposes over the centuries, including a fortress, a papal residence, and a prison. Night tours of Castel Sant'Angelo often include access to its upper terraces, which offer panoramic views of Rome's illuminated skyline. The sight of St. Peter's Basilica glowing softly in the distance is nothing short of breathtaking. Inside, the museum's exhibits, ranging from ancient artifacts to Renaissance frescoes, take on a new dimension when viewed in the quieter, more intimate setting of the evening.

Another unique perspective of Rome at night can be enjoyed from the Tiber River. Evening boat tours offer a relaxing and picturesque way to see the city's landmarks from the water. As you glide along the river, you'll pass under historic bridges like Ponte Sant'Angelo and catch glimpses of landmarks such as the Vatican and the Trastevere neighborhood. The gentle movement of the boat, combined with the shimmering reflections of lights on the water, creates a tranquil and romantic atmosphere. Some tours even include dinner or live music, adding an extra layer of enjoyment to the experience.

For those who prefer to explore on foot, Rome's Jewish Ghetto offers a fascinating and atmospheric night tour. This historic neighborhood, known for its rich cultural heritage and culinary traditions, comes alive in a different way after dark. Guided tours often highlight the area's history, from its origins in ancient Rome to its more recent past, while also showcasing its architectural and culinary delights. The quiet streets, illuminated by soft streetlights, create a sense of intimacy that enhances the storytelling. A visit to the Portico of Octavia and the Great Synagogue, beautifully lit at night, provides a poignant reminder of the neighborhood's enduring spirit.

Rome's night tours are not only about history and architecture but also about experiencing the city's vibrant culture and energy. Food and wine tours, for example, combine the best of Rome's culinary scene with its nighttime charm. These tours often start with a visit to a local market or food shop, followed by stops at traditional trattorias, wine bars, and gelaterias. Along the way, guides share stories about Rome's food traditions and the role of dining in Italian culture. The combination of delicious flavors, warm hospitality, and the city's illuminated streets creates an experience that is both satisfying and unforgettable.

The magic of Rome at night lies in its ability to reveal new layers of beauty, history, and emotion. Whether you're walking through ancient ruins, exploring underground catacombs, or simply enjoying a gelato by the Trevi Fountain, the city's nocturnal charm is impossible to resist. Night tours offer a unique perspective that complements and enriches the daytime experience, allowing you to see Rome in a way that is both timeless and deeply personal. As the city's lights flicker and its streets grow quieter, the Eternal City invites you to lose yourself in its stories, its beauty, and its enduring allure.

Special Events and Festivals: Rome's Nightlife Calendar

Rome, a city that thrives on history, culture, and celebration, extends its vibrant energy into the night with an array of special events and festivals that punctuate the calendar year. These nighttime gatherings are not mere sideshows but integral parts of Roman life, blending tradition, art, music, and a deep sense of community. Whether you're a visitor eager to immerse yourself in the city's unique atmosphere or a local looking for a reason to revel, the Eternal City offers countless opportunities to experience its festive spirit under the stars. From religious celebrations steeped in history to modern cultural festivals that draw international crowds, Rome's nightlife calendar is as dynamic as the city itself.

One of the most anticipated annual events in Rome is the Festa di San Giovanni, a celebration in honor of St. John the Baptist, the city's co-patron saint. Held on the evening of June 23rd, this festival brings Romans together in Piazza San Giovanni, where food, music, and dance take center stage. The piazza is transformed into a lively spectacle, with street vendors serving traditional Roman dishes such as lumache (snails), a delicacy associated with the festival. As live music fills the air, locals and visitors alike join in dancing, creating a joyful atmosphere that continues late into the night. The event culminates with a spectacular fireworks display, illuminating the iconic façade of the Basilica of St. John Lateran. The Festa di San Giovanni is a perfect example of how Rome intertwines its religious heritage with communal celebration, offering a glimpse into the city's enduring traditions.

For art and history enthusiasts, the Notte dei Musei, or Night of the Museums, is a must-attend event. Held annually in May, this initiative allows visitors to explore Rome's museums, galleries, and archaeological sites after dark, often for free or at a reduced cost. Major landmarks such as the Capitoline Museums, the Vatican Museums, and the MAXXI Museum of Contemporary Art extend their hours, offering special exhibitions, live performances, and guided tours. Wandering through the halls of these institutions at night, free from the usual daytime crowds, provides an entirely different perspective on Rome's artistic and cultural treasures. The dim lighting and hushed atmosphere add an almost magical quality, making the experience both intimate and awe-inspiring.

Summer in Rome is synonymous with the Estate Romana, a citywide festival that spans the warmer months and brings the streets, piazzas, and parks to life with a dazzling array of events. Among the highlights of this festival are the outdoor cinema screenings held in historic locations such as Piazza Vittorio and the Tiber Island. Watching a classic Italian film or a contemporary blockbuster under the stars, with Rome's architectural marvels as your backdrop, is an experience that captures the essence of summer in the city. Estate Romana also features open-air concerts, theater performances, and food festivals, ensuring there's something for everyone to enjoy. The festival's diversity reflects Rome's multifaceted identity, blending its rich history with its modern, cosmopolitan spirit.

Music lovers will find plenty to celebrate in Rome's nightlife calendar, particularly during the Roma Summer Fest. Hosted at the Auditorium Parco della Musica, this annual event attracts world-renowned artists and bands, spanning genres from classical and jazz to rock and pop. The open-air cavea, or amphitheater, provides an intimate setting for these performances, with the warm summer breeze and the twinkling city lights enhancing the experience. Past lineups have included legendary acts such as Elton John, Leonard Cohen, and Ennio Morricone, making the Roma Summer Fest a highlight of the city's cultural calendar. For those who prefer a more underground vibe, the Rock in Roma festival, held at the Ippodromo delle Capannelle, offers a grittier, high-energy alternative. With its eclectic mix of international and local talent, Rock in Roma has become a magnet for music enthusiasts looking to immerse themselves in the city's vibrant nightlife.

Religious festivals also play a significant role in shaping Rome's nighttime events, with the Natale di Roma, or Rome's Birthday, standing out as one of the most spectacular. Celebrated on April 21st, this event marks the legendary founding of the city in 753 BC. The festivities often include historical reenactments, parades, and fireworks, with many activities taking place after sunset. The Colosseum and the Roman Forum serve as focal points for the celebrations, their ancient stones illuminated by dramatic lighting that emphasizes their grandeur. One of the most memorable aspects of Natale di Roma is the nighttime procession of gladiators, centurions, and Vestal Virgins, who march through the city's streets in full costume. The combination of history, pageantry, and the city's timeless beauty makes this event a truly unforgettable experience.

Rome's culinary culture takes center stage during events like Taste of Roma, an annual food festival that showcases the city's finest chefs and restaurants. Held in September at the Auditorium Parco della Musica, this festival invites food lovers to sample gourmet dishes, attend cooking demonstrations, and participate in wine tastings. While the event runs throughout the day, the evening hours offer a particularly enchanting experience. The venue's outdoor spaces are illuminated with fairy lights, creating a festive atmosphere that complements the culinary delights on offer. Taste of Roma is more than just a food festival; it's a celebration of Rome's gastronomic heritage and its innovative culinary scene, making it a highlight of the city's nightlife calendar.

During the Christmas season, Rome's nightlife takes on a magical quality, with events and festivities that capture the spirit of the holidays. The Piazza Navona Christmas Market is a beloved tradition, offering an array of stalls selling handcrafted ornaments, toys, and seasonal treats. While the market is bustling during the day, it becomes particularly enchanting at night, when the square is illuminated by twinkling lights and the Fountain of the Four Rivers glistens in the cold winter air. Christmas concerts, often held in historic churches such as Santa Maria in Aracoeli and Sant'Ignazio, provide a serene and spiritual counterpoint to the festive hustle and bustle. These performances, featuring traditional carols and classical music, create a sense of peace and reverence that resonates deeply with both locals and visitors.

For a more modern take on holiday celebrations, the New Year's Eve festivities in Rome are an unmissable event. The city hosts a range of parties, concerts, and fireworks displays, with the main celebrations centered around the Circus Maximus. This ancient chariot racing stadium transforms into a massive open-air venue, featuring live music, dance performances, and a midnight fireworks show that lights up the Roman skyline. The atmosphere is electric, as thousands of revelers come together to ring in the new year with joy and excitement. For a more intimate celebration, many of Rome's rooftop bars and restaurants offer special New Year's Eve menus, complete with champagne toasts and panoramic views of the city's illuminated landmarks.

Film enthusiasts will appreciate the Festa del Cinema di Roma, or Rome Film Festival, which takes place in October. While the festival's screenings and events run throughout the day, the evening premieres and red-carpet events are where the glamour truly shines. Held at the Auditorium Parco della Musica, the festival attracts international stars, directors, and film lovers, making it a focal point of Rome's cultural scene. The outdoor screenings, often set against the backdrop of the venue's striking architecture, provide a unique way to experience cinema under the stars. The Rome Film Festival is not just about movies; it's a celebration of storytelling, creativity, and the city's enduring love affair with the arts.

Rome's nightlife calendar is as diverse and dynamic as the city itself, offering a wealth of opportunities to celebrate, connect, and immerse yourself in its vibrant culture. Whether you're dancing in Piazza San Giovanni, marveling at the Colosseum during Natale di Roma, or savoring gourmet dishes at Taste of Roma, each event provides a unique window into the city's soul. These special occasions are more than just dates on a calendar; they are moments that bring people together, creating memories that linger long after the festivities have ended. In Rome, the night is not simply a time to rest—it's a time to revel, to discover, and to embrace the magic of a city that never ceases to inspire.

CHAPTER 7: FINAL TIPS AND RESOURCES

How to Avoid Travel Burnout in Rome

Exploring Rome can feel like stepping into a living museum, where every corner reveals a new treasure, and every cobblestone street has a story to tell. The grandeur of the Colosseum, the majesty of St. Peter's Basilica, and the timeless charm of its piazzas can overwhelm even the most seasoned traveler. While the city's allure is undeniable, the sheer abundance of sights, sounds, and experiences can also lead to travel burnout if you're not careful. The fatigue of trying to see it all, paired with the physical demands of navigating a bustling city on foot, can dull the magic of your visit. However, with a thoughtful approach and some practical strategies, you can enjoy Rome without feeling exhausted or overstimulated.

Pacing yourself is one of the most effective ways to avoid burnout when exploring Rome. The temptation to cram as much as possible into each day is understandable, especially in a city with such a wealth of attractions. Yet, trying to visit multiple major landmarks in rapid succession can quickly leave you drained. Instead of attempting to conquer the Colosseum, Vatican Museums, and Roman Forum all in one day, spread these iconic sites across several days. Create a loose itinerary that balances high-energy activities with more relaxed ones. For example, follow a morning spent exploring the bustling Vatican Museums with an afternoon unwinding in the peaceful gardens of Villa Borghese. This approach allows you to fully savor each experience without feeling rushed or overwhelmed.

Taking breaks throughout the day is essential. Rome's streets are charming but can be physically demanding, with uneven cobblestones, steep hills, and a layout that often forces you to walk longer than anticipated. Building time into your schedule to rest and recharge can make all the difference. Seek out shaded benches in the city's many picturesque piazzas, or step into a quiet church to escape the hustle and bustle for a few moments. Churches like Santa Maria in Trastevere or Sant'Ignazio di Loyola not only provide a tranquil retreat but also offer stunning interiors to admire while you rest. Even a brief pause to sit at a café with an espresso or gelato can help you reset before continuing your explorations.

Staying hydrated and nourished is equally important. Rome's Mediterranean climate, especially in the summer months, can be unforgiving, with high temperatures and intense sun. Carry a reusable water bottle and take advantage of the city's nasoni—public drinking fountains that provide fresh, cool water. These fountains, scattered throughout Rome, are a lifesaver for weary travelers. When it comes to meals, resist the urge to grab quick bites on the go. Instead, embrace the Italian tradition of leisurely dining. A sit-down lunch at a trattoria is not only an opportunity to experience authentic Roman cuisine but also a chance to rest before tackling your afternoon plans. Dishes like cacio e pepe or a simple caprese salad paired with a glass of house wine can reinvigorate both your body and spirit.

Choosing accommodations in a central location can significantly reduce travel fatigue. Staying in neighborhoods like Campo de' Fiori, Trastevere, or Monti places you within walking distance of many key attractions, eliminating the need for long commutes. While Rome's public transportation system is extensive, it can be crowded and unpredictable, adding unnecessary stress to your day. Being able to return to your hotel or apartment for a midday break or to drop off shopping bags makes a world of difference. A brief rest in the comfort of your accommodations can recharge your energy and help you avoid the feeling of being constantly on the go.

Learning to prioritize your must-see attractions is another crucial step in avoiding burnout. Rome is a city where it's impossible to see everything in one trip, and accepting this reality can help you focus on what truly matters to you. Whether it's ancient history, Renaissance art, or culinary delights, tailor your itinerary to align with your interests. If the thought of navigating the crowds at the Vatican Museums feels daunting, consider skipping it in favor of smaller, less crowded gems like the Galleria Doria Pamphilj or the Capitoline Museums. By choosing quality over quantity, you'll have more meaningful and memorable experiences.

Allowing time for spontaneity can also enhance your trip and prevent exhaustion. While having a plan is helpful, leaving room for unplanned moments can lead to some of the most rewarding experiences. Wander through a neighborhood you hadn't intended to visit, stop at a shop that catches your eye, or linger over a glass of wine at a sidewalk café. These unscripted adventures often provide a much-needed break from the structure of an itinerary and allow you to connect with Rome in a more personal and relaxed way.

Avoiding peak hours at major attractions can save you both time and energy. Many of Rome's iconic sites are busiest in the late morning and early afternoon, with long lines and large crowds. Arriving early in the morning or later in the evening not only reduces wait times but also allows you to experience these landmarks in a more serene atmosphere. For instance, a visit to the Trevi Fountain at dawn offers a completely different experience than the midday crush of tourists. Similarly, evening tours of the Colosseum or Vatican Museums provide a quieter, more intimate perspective on these world-famous sites.

Engaging with local culture can be a refreshing way to balance sightseeing with deeper connections. Instead of rushing from one tourist attraction to the next, take the time to participate in activities that immerse you in Roman life. Attend a cooking class to learn how to make fresh pasta, join a wine tasting to explore Italy's renowned vintages, or visit a local market like

Campo de' Fiori to sample regional specialties. These experiences not only provide a break from the physical demands of sightseeing but also enrich your understanding of Rome's culture and traditions.

Embracing the slower pace of Roman evenings can be a wonderful antidote to daytime activity. After a day of exploring, allow yourself to unwind with a leisurely dinner or a stroll through the city's illuminated streets. Rome at night is a different world, with its landmarks beautifully lit and its piazzas alive with the hum of conversation. Sitting at a café in Piazza Navona or wandering along the Tiber River under the soft glow of streetlights can help you decompress and appreciate the city's beauty in a more relaxed way.

Listening to your body and knowing when to rest is perhaps the most important aspect of avoiding travel burnout. It's easy to get caught up in the excitement of being in Rome and feel the need to keep going, but pushing yourself too hard can diminish your enjoyment of the experience. If you wake up feeling particularly tired, give yourself permission to take a slower day. Spend the morning reading in a quiet park, visit a less demanding attraction, or simply enjoy the luxury of doing nothing for a while. Remember that part of the joy of travel is allowing yourself to be present in the moment, rather than constantly striving to check items off a list.

Rome is a city that rewards those who take the time to truly absorb its essence. By pacing yourself, staying mindful of your needs, and embracing the city's relaxed rhythm, you can experience the best of what it has to offer without succumbing to fatigue. Travel burnout doesn't have to be part of your journey; with a thoughtful approach, you can leave Rome feeling inspired, enriched, and eager to return for more.

Souvenirs Worth Bringing Home

Rome, with its timeless charm, is more than just a destination—it's a city that leaves an indelible mark on those who visit. Its cobblestone streets, ancient ruins, and culinary delights often evoke a deep desire to take a piece of the Eternal City home with you. Souvenirs are not merely tokens of a trip; they are tangible memories, reminders of moments, stories, and experiences that transport you back to the vibrancy of Roman life. However, the challenge lies in choosing items that truly capture the essence of the city and hold lasting value, rather than falling into the trap of kitschy trinkets that may lose their appeal once unpacked. Rome offers a wealth of meaningful and authentic souvenirs, each reflecting a slice of its rich culture and history.

A bottle of Italian olive oil, especially one sourced from the Lazio region surrounding Rome, makes for a practical and quintessentially Italian souvenir. The olive oil produced here is often of exceptional quality, with a distinct flavor profile that speaks to the fertile soil and Mediterranean climate. Small shops and specialty stores, such as Roscioli or Volpetti, stock a curated selection of premium extra virgin olive oils, often hand-labeled by local producers. These oils are perfect for drizzling over fresh bread, dressing salads, or recreating Italian recipes at home. To elevate the gift, consider pairing the oil with a bottle of aged balsamic vinegar or even a small package of dried pasta, creating a thoughtful culinary set that will evoke the flavors of Rome with every use.

For food enthusiasts, cured meats and cheeses offer a delectable way to bring a taste of Rome back home. Guanciale, a type of cured pork cheek, is a staple in Roman cuisine and the key ingredient in iconic dishes like carbonara and amatriciana. While transporting fresh meats internationally can be tricky, vacuum-sealed packages of guanciale are often available at gourmet food shops and are designed to travel well. Similarly, aged Pecorino Romano cheese, with its salty and tangy profile, is a versatile souvenir that can enhance a variety of dishes. Be sure to check customs regulations in your home country before purchasing perishable items, but when permitted, these culinary treasures are as authentic as it gets.

Rome's coffee culture is another defining aspect of the city, and bringing home a bag of Italian coffee is an excellent way to relive those moments spent sipping espresso at a bustling bar. Tazza d'Oro and Sant'Eustachio Il Caffè are two beloved local institutions that sell their signature coffee blends, often roasted in-house for maximum freshness. The distinctive aroma of Italian coffee can instantly transport you back to the piazzas and cobblestone alleys where you first fell in love with the city. Pair your coffee purchase with a stovetop Moka pot, a quintessential tool for brewing espresso at home, and you've got the perfect combination for recreating the Roman coffee experience.

Artisanal leather goods are another category of souvenirs that reflect Rome's dedication to craftsmanship and tradition. From belts and wallets to handbags and gloves, leather products made in Italy are renowned for their quality and durability. Shops like Campo Marzio and leather artisans scattered throughout the city offer items that are both functional and stylish, often crafted by hand using age-old techniques. A leather-bound journal, for instance, not only makes for a practical keepsake but also serves as a vessel for jotting down your memories of Rome. The smooth texture of the leather and the rich aroma will serve as a lasting reminder of the time you spent wandering the city.

For those with an appreciation for history and art, Rome's abundance of museums and archaeological sites inspires a range of unique souvenirs. Reproductions of ancient Roman coins or busts, available at museum gift shops like those at the Capitoline Museums or the Vatican Museums, allow you to take home a small piece of the city's storied past. These replicas are often crafted with meticulous attention to detail, making them ideal for history buffs or anyone looking to add a touch of antiquity to their home décor. Similarly, prints of famous artworks, such as those by Caravaggio or Raphael, serve as elegant mementos of your visit to Rome's artistic treasures.

Religious souvenirs hold a special place in Rome, particularly for those who have visited the Vatican. Rosaries, crucifixes, and medals bearing images of saints are widely available and come in a range of materials, from simple wooden beads to ornate designs in silver or gold. Many of these items can be purchased at shops near St. Peter's Basilica or directly within the Vatican itself. What makes these religious souvenirs even more meaningful is the opportunity to have them blessed by a priest, either during a Mass or at a private audience. This added personal touch imbues the items with spiritual significance, making them cherished keepsakes for years to come.

Jewelry lovers will find plenty of options in Rome, from high-end boutiques on Via Condotti to local artisans crafting handmade pieces. One particularly distinctive souvenir is the micromosaic jewelry for which Italy is famous. These intricate designs, made from tiny pieces of colored glass or stone, often depict Roman landmarks, floral patterns, or religious symbols. A pair of micromosaic earrings or a pendant can serve as a wearable reminder of your trip while showcasing a unique aspect of Italian artistry. Alternatively, look for cameo jewelry, another Italian specialty, featuring carved images set against contrasting backgrounds.

Rome's love affair with literature and the written word is evident in its many bookstores, some of which offer beautiful editions of Italian classics. A copy of Dante's "Divine Comedy" or a collection of Roman myths and legends, especially if printed in Italian, can serve as a meaningful souvenir for book lovers. For something more contemporary, consider a travelogue or novel set in Rome, allowing you to relive the city's magic through the eyes of a storyteller. Some bookstores, like Libreria del Viaggiatore, specialize in travel-related books, offering a curated selection that captures the spirit of exploration.

Ceramics and pottery, often hand-painted with traditional Italian motifs, are another excellent option for souvenirs. Plates, bowls, and decorative tiles featuring vibrant colors and intricate patterns make for practical yet beautiful keepsakes. Shops in Rome's Trastevere neighborhood often stock these items, many of which are made in nearby regions like Umbria or Tuscany. A ceramic piece can brighten up your home while serving as a functional reminder of your Roman holiday.

Perfumes and soaps, crafted by local apothecaries, offer a sensory way to remember your time in Rome. Santa Maria Novella, one of the oldest pharmacies in the world, produces a range of fragrances, skincare products, and herbal remedies that make for luxurious gifts. The scents, often inspired by the Italian countryside, evoke memories of orange groves, lavender fields, and Mediterranean breezes. A bottle of perfume or a bar of handmade soap is a small but meaningful way to encapsulate the essence of Rome.

Finally, for something truly unique, consider seeking out vintage items or antiques at Rome's markets. The Porta Portese flea market, held every Sunday, is a treasure trove of curiosities, from vintage postcards and antique jewelry to old books and decorative trinkets. Each item carries its own story, adding an element of history and character to your collection of souvenirs. Whether you're drawn to a whimsical piece of vintage clothing or a well-worn piece of furniture, the thrill of discovering something one-of-a-kind makes the experience all the more rewarding.

Souvenirs from Rome are more than just objects; they are gateways to memories, emotions, and stories. Choosing items that resonate with your personal experience of the city ensures that they will hold meaning long after your trip has ended.

With every sip of Italian coffee, every glance at a piece of jewelry, or every taste of olive oil, you'll be transported back to the vibrant streets, sunlit piazzas, and timeless beauty of the Eternal City. In Rome, even the simplest memento can carry a world of meaning, creating a connection between you and the city that lasts a lifetime.

Emergency Contacts and Local Support

Navigating a foreign city as rich, sprawling, and culturally immersive as Rome can be an exhilarating experience. However, the unpredictability of travel means that emergencies, big or small, can arise. Whether it's a lost passport, a sudden medical issue, or simply needing assistance with directions, having access to the right emergency contacts and local support systems can transform a stressful situation into a manageable one. Preparation is key when it comes to ensuring your safety and peace of mind while exploring the Eternal City. With a mix of historical charm and modern infrastructure, Rome offers a variety of services and resources that cater to travelers in need of assistance. Knowing how to access these resources can save time, reduce anxiety, and help you get back to enjoying your adventure.

The most critical number to remember when in Rome, or anywhere in Italy, is 112, the European emergency number. This universal number connects you to a central dispatcher capable of directing your call to the appropriate emergency service, whether it be police, ambulance, or fire brigade. Operators are often multilingual, and in a city as international as Rome, English-speaking support is readily available. If you're unsure which service you need, calling 112 ensures you'll be guided to the right one. It's also worth noting that Italy has specialized numbers for specific emergencies: 113 for police, 115 for fire services, and 118 for medical emergencies.

While these numbers are still in use, 112 simplifies the process by acting as a one-stop solution.

Health-related emergencies can be particularly daunting when you're in a foreign country. Rome's healthcare system, however, is robust and accessible to tourists. If you require urgent medical attention, dialing 118 will connect you to emergency medical services. Trained operators will assess your situation and dispatch an ambulance if necessary. Rome is home to several well-equipped hospitals, including Policlinico Umberto I, the city's largest public hospital, and Ospedale San Camillo-Forlanini, known for its high standard of care. Many hospitals have English-speaking staff or translators available to assist international patients. For less critical medical issues, pharmacies, or "farmacie," are a convenient first point of contact. Easily recognizable by their green cross signs, pharmacies in Rome often have licensed pharmacists who can provide advice, over-the-counter medications, or direct you to a doctor if needed.

Travelers should also be aware of Guardia Medica Turistica, a medical service specifically designed for tourists. These clinics are staffed with doctors who are accustomed to assisting international visitors and can handle minor medical concerns. While services are not free, the fees are generally reasonable, and they often accept a variety of payment methods. To locate the nearest Guardia Medica Turistica, your hotel concierge or a local pharmacy can provide guidance. Additionally, keeping a small first-aid kit with essentials such as bandages, pain relievers, and any personal medications can be invaluable for addressing minor issues without the need for professional care.

Lost or stolen passports are another common travel dilemma that can disrupt plans. If you find yourself in this situation, your first step should be to file a report with the local police, or "Carabinieri." You can visit any police station, or "Questura," to make the report, which is a necessary document for obtaining a replacement passport. For U.S. citizens, the U.S. Embassy in Rome is located near Villa Borghese at Via Vittorio Veneto, 121. The embassy provides support for lost or stolen passports, as well as other consular services. Other embassies and consulates, such as those for the UK, Canada, and Australia, are similarly located within the city and offer comparable services. It's always a good idea to keep digital and physical copies of your passport and other important documents to streamline the replacement process.

Rome's public transportation system, while efficient, can sometimes lead to confusion, especially for first-time visitors. If you find yourself lost or needing assistance with transport, the ATAC offices, which manage public transit in the city, can provide help. Located at major transit hubs like Termini Station, these offices have staff who can offer directions, maps, and information about buses, trams, and metro lines. For real-time updates and route planning, the MyCicero app is a valuable tool that covers Rome's transportation network. Additionally, taxi services in Rome are reliable, and official taxis are white with the "TAXI" sign on top. If you feel unsafe or unsure about your route, hailing a taxi or using a trusted ride-hailing app like Free Now can quickly get you back on track.

Language barriers can sometimes pose challenges when seeking help, but Rome's status as a global tourist destination means that English is widely spoken in areas frequented by visitors. Restaurants, hotels, and major attractions often have English-speaking staff. However, in more residential neighborhoods or less tourist-centric parts of the city, you might encounter fewer English speakers. To bridge the gap, downloading a reliable translation app can be incredibly useful. Apps like Google Translate allow you to type or speak phrases, and the app will provide translations in Italian. Learning a few basic Italian phrases, such as "Dov'è il bagno?" (Where is the bathroom?) or "Mi sono perso" (I'm lost), can also go a long way in facilitating communication.

Rome's abundant network of tourist information centers is another excellent resource for visitors. These centers, operated by Roma Capitale, are strategically located at key points across the city, including Fiumicino Airport, Piazza Venezia, and Termini Station. Staffed with knowledgeable personnel, these centers provide maps, brochures, and advice on everything from sightseeing to emergency contacts. If you're unsure where to turn for help, a tourist information center is often a good starting point.

Credit card issues, such as a lost or blocked card, can cause significant inconvenience during your trip. Most international banks have helplines with 24/7 customer service to assist in such situations. It's wise to carry a backup card or some cash in euros to cover immediate expenses while resolving the issue. Many Italian ATMs, or "bancomat," allow you to withdraw cash using a card from your home country, though it's essential to be aware of any fees or restrictions your bank may impose. Notifying your bank of your travel dates before your trip can help prevent your card from being flagged for unusual activity.

If your situation requires legal assistance, Rome has a network of lawyers who specialize in helping international clients. The U.S. Embassy and other consulates maintain lists of local attorneys who speak English and have experience working with foreigners. Whether you're dealing with a legal dispute, an accident, or other issues requiring legal advice, these professionals can guide you through the process and ensure your rights are protected.

Travel insurance is another layer of security that can provide financial and logistical support during emergencies. Comprehensive travel insurance policies often cover medical expenses, trip cancellations, and lost belongings, giving you peace of mind while exploring Rome. If you need to make a claim, having documentation such as receipts, police reports, and medical records will streamline the process. Many insurance providers also offer 24/7 helplines to assist with emergencies, ensuring you're never left to navigate challenges alone.

Finally, don't underestimate the power of local kindness. Romans are known for their warmth and hospitality, and many are willing to assist travelers in need. Whether it's a shopkeeper helping you find your way, a fellow passenger offering advice on public transport, or a waiter recommending a pharmacy nearby, the people of Rome are often among the most valuable resources you'll encounter.

Being prepared with a comprehensive list of emergency contacts and local support options ensures that you can handle unexpected situations with confidence. Rome's blend of ancient charm and modern infrastructure offers a safety net for travelers, making it easier to navigate challenges and focus on the joy of discovery. By taking simple precautions and knowing where to turn for help, you can explore the Eternal City with peace of mind, ready to embrace all the wonders it has to offer.

Recommended Books and Movies About Rome

Rome has inspired countless authors, filmmakers, and storytellers across centuries, each drawn to its rich history, unparalleled beauty, and vibrant culture. From ancient times to the modern era, the city has served as both a muse and a setting for narratives that explore its profound influence on the world. Books and movies about Rome not only deepen one's appreciation of the city but also prepare travelers to experience it with more insight and context. Whether delving into its ancient past, marveling at its Renaissance rebirth, or exploring its modern complexities, these works of art capture the essence of Rome and bring it vividly to life.

One of the most enduring texts about Rome is Edward Gibbon's monumental work, *The History of the Decline and Fall of the Roman Empire*. Written in the 18th century, this exhaustive account of Rome's transition from the height of its imperial power to its eventual downfall remains a cornerstone of historical literature. Gibbon's writing is both meticulous and evocative, providing readers with a deep understanding of the political, social, and cultural forces that shaped the empire. While the length of the book may be daunting, its insights into the grandeur and complexity of ancient Rome make it an essential read for anyone seeking to grasp the city's historical significance.

For a more personal and poetic exploration of Rome, Elizabeth Bowen's *A Time in Rome* offers a beautifully written account of the author's time spent wandering the city in the mid-20th century. Bowen's observations are sharp and insightful, capturing the layers of history that coexist in Rome's streets and monuments. Her reflections often weave between the ancient and the contemporary, offering readers a sense of the timelessness that defines the city. The book reads like a love letter to Rome, filled with vivid descriptions and thoughtful musings that make it a perfect companion for those preparing to visit.

Robert Graves' *I, Claudius* and its sequel, *Claudius the God*, bring ancient Rome to life through the fictionalized memoirs of Emperor Claudius. These novels, set during the tumultuous years of the Julio-Claudian dynasty, provide a gripping portrayal of political intrigue, betrayal, and power struggles. Graves' storytelling is masterful, blending historical accuracy with imaginative flair to create characters that feel both larger-than-life and deeply human. The books transport readers to the heart of imperial Rome, offering a perspective that is at once entertaining and enlightening.

Alberto Angela's *A Day in the Life of Ancient Rome* takes readers on an immersive journey through the daily routines of

Romans living during the height of the empire. Angela's attention to detail and engaging narrative style make this book a fascinating exploration of topics ranging from food and fashion to politics and religion. By focusing on the lives of ordinary citizens as well as the elite, Angela provides a well-rounded view of what it was like to live in ancient Rome. The book's vivid descriptions and approachable tone make it an excellent choice for those looking to gain a deeper understanding of Roman culture.

Modern Rome also finds its voice in literature, with works like Anthony Doerr's *Four Seasons in Rome*. This memoir chronicles the author's year-long residency in the city, offering a delightful blend of personal anecdotes and observations about Roman life. Doerr's lyrical prose captures the beauty of Rome's landscapes, the quirks of its people, and the rhythms of its seasons. The book's intimate perspective makes it relatable for anyone who has ever fallen under the spell of Rome or dreams of doing so.

When it comes to cinema, Rome has been the backdrop for some of the most iconic films in cinematic history. Federico Fellini's *La Dolce Vita* is a masterpiece that captures the glamour, decadence, and existential ennui of post-war Rome. The film follows journalist Marcello Rubini as he navigates the city's elite social circles, encountering a cast of unforgettable characters along the way. Fellini's vision of Rome is both alluring and haunting, reflecting the contradictions that define the city. The film's iconic scenes—such as Anita Ekberg wading into the Trevi Fountain—have become emblematic of Roman sensuality and allure.

Another classic is William Wyler's *Roman Holiday*, a romantic comedy that introduced the world to the charm of Audrey Hepburn. The film tells the story of a young princess who escapes her royal duties for a day of adventure in Rome, accompanied by an American journalist played by Gregory Peck. Shot on location, the film showcases many of the city's landmarks, including the Spanish Steps, the Colosseum, and Piazza Venezia. Its lighthearted tone and picturesque imagery make it a delightful introduction to Rome's timeless appeal.

Paolo Sorrentino's *The Great Beauty* offers a more contemporary and introspective view of Rome. The film follows Jep Gambardella, a writer and socialite, as he reflects on his life and the city that has shaped it. Sorrentino's Rome is a city of contrasts, where opulence and decay coexist, and beauty can be found in both the grandiose and the mundane. The film's stunning cinematography captures Rome in all its glory, from its historic landmarks to its hidden corners, making it a visual feast for viewers.

For those interested in ancient Rome, Ridley Scott's *Gladiator* provides a gripping portrayal of the empire's grandeur and brutality. While the film takes historical liberties, it effectively conveys the spectacle and drama of Roman life, particularly through its depiction of the Colosseum's gladiatorial games. Russell Crowe's performance as Maximus, a betrayed general seeking vengeance, adds emotional depth to the story, while the film's epic scale brings the world of ancient Rome to life.

On a lighter note, Woody Allen's *To Rome with Love* offers a series of vignettes that highlight the city's romantic and whimsical side. The film's ensemble cast and interconnected stories explore themes of love, ambition, and the magic of chance encounters. While not as profound as some of the other films on this list, it captures the charm and unpredictability of life in Rome.

For documentaries, *Rome: Engineering an Empire* delves into the architectural and engineering marvels that defined ancient Rome. Through detailed reconstructions and expert commentary, the documentary examines structures like the aqueducts, the Colosseum, and the Pantheon, offering viewers a deeper appreciation of Rome's innovations. It's an excellent resource for history enthusiasts or anyone curious about the city's enduring legacy.

Literature and film have a unique ability to transport us, offering glimpses into worlds that might otherwise be inaccessible. The works mentioned above serve as windows into Rome's many facets, from its ancient origins to its modern vibrancy. They enrich our understanding of the city, allowing us to connect with it on a deeper level. Whether you're preparing for a trip or simply dreaming of the Eternal City, these books and movies provide a rich tapestry of stories that capture the essence of Rome. The beauty of Rome lies not only in its physical presence but also in the countless ways it has inspired creativity, making it a city that continues to resonate across time and mediums.

Farewell to the Eternal City: Leaving with Lasting Memories

The final hours in Rome, those bittersweet moments when you know your time in the Eternal City is coming to an end, can be some of the most poignant of your journey. Rome has a way of embedding itself deeply into your senses—its golden light reflecting on ancient ruins, the aroma of freshly brewed espresso wafting through its cobblestone streets, the distant hum of church bells mingling with the chatter of locals. Leaving this city, so layered with history and emotion, feels less like closing a chapter and more like saying goodbye to an old friend. Yet, a farewell to Rome doesn't have to mean leaving it behind entirely. With the right mindset and a few thoughtful actions, you can ensure that the memories you've created here remain vivid, serving as a lasting connection to this remarkable place.

One of the most meaningful ways to solidify your memories of Rome is to revisit your favorite spots before you leave.

Whether it's a piazza where you lingered over a gelato, a quiet corner of the Roman Forum where you felt the weight of history, or a tiny trattoria where you tasted the best cacio e pepe of your life, returning to these places allows you to soak in their atmosphere one last time. Without the pressure of an itinerary, you can experience them with a sense of calm and reflection, noticing details you might have overlooked before. The light might hit the Trevi Fountain differently in the morning than it did at night, or the rhythm of life in Campo de' Fiori might feel slower and more intimate as vendors pack up their stalls for the day. These final visits become a way of imprinting these places onto your memory, ensuring they'll remain with you long after you've boarded your flight.

Taking the time to savor one last meal in Rome can be a deeply satisfying way to bid the city farewell. Roman cuisine, rooted in tradition and simplicity, is as much a part of the city's identity as its monuments. Seek out a restaurant that embodies the authentic spirit of Rome, whether it's a family-run osteria tucked away in Trastevere or a bustling pizzeria in Testaccio. Order the dishes that have become your favorites during your stay, or try something you haven't yet had the chance to experience. Let the flavors linger, and take in the ambiance of the restaurant—the clinking of glasses, the laughter of diners, the warmth of the candlelight. These sensory details will stay with you, serving as a reminder of the moments of joy and connection that food can create.

Writing about your experiences in Rome can help preserve them in vivid detail. Whether it's a travel journal, a series of notes on your phone, or even a collection of postcards you've written to yourself, putting your thoughts and observations into words allows you to process and reflect on your time in the city. What surprised you most about Rome? What moments took your breath away? Was there an interaction with a local that stood out, or a hidden gem you stumbled upon that felt like your own secret discovery? These personal reflections, captured in your own voice, will become a treasure trove of memories that you can revisit whenever you feel the pull of nostalgia.

Shopping for a final souvenir can be a meaningful way to take a piece of Rome home with you. While you may have already picked up a few mementos during your stay, this last purchase can carry special significance. Perhaps it's a hand-painted ceramic dish from a shop in Trastevere, a bottle of olive oil from a local market, or a leather-bound notebook from a traditional artisan. Choose something that resonates with your experience of the city, something that will evoke its essence every time you see or use it. These items, infused with the spirit of Rome, can serve as touchstones to your memories, transporting you back to its streets and piazzas in an instant.

Photographs, though ubiquitous in the age of smartphones, remain one of the most powerful ways to capture the beauty of a place. As you prepare to leave Rome, consider taking a final walk with the sole purpose of photographing the city. Focus not only on its grand landmarks but also on its quieter, more intimate details—the ivy climbing up the walls of a weathered building, the pattern of cobblestones beneath your feet, the way the light filters through the trees in Villa Borghese. These images, taken with intention and care, will form a visual narrative of your time in Rome, allowing you to relive its magic through your own perspective.

Saying goodbye to the people you've met in Rome, whether they're fellow travelers, local hosts, or newfound friends, can be an emotional yet fulfilling part of leaving. If you've formed connections during your stay, take a moment to express your gratitude and exchange contact information. A heartfelt conversation or a simple note of thanks can leave a lasting impression, and these relationships may continue to enrich your life long after you've returned home. Staying in touch with the people you've met can also serve as a bridge back to Rome, keeping its spirit alive in your everyday life.

Reflecting on the lessons you've learned in Rome can add depth to your farewell. The city, with its layers of history and its vibrant present, has a way of teaching its visitors about resilience, beauty, and the art of savoring life. What has Rome taught you? Perhaps it's the value of slowing down and enjoying a leisurely meal, the resilience of structures that have stood for millennia, or the joy of wandering without a set destination. These lessons, carried with you, become part of the legacy of your time in Rome, enriching your perspective and shaping your approach to life.

As you make your way to the airport or train station, take a moment to look out at the city one last time. The domes, the rooftops, the ancient ruins in the distance—they are not just a backdrop to your trip but a part of your story now. The sense of belonging that Rome cultivates in its visitors is one of its greatest gifts, and even as you leave, you carry a piece of it with you. The Eternal City, true to its name, remains eternal in your heart, a place you can return to in memory, in dreams, or one day, in person.

Planning how you'll keep Rome alive in your daily life can ease the sadness of leaving. This might mean cooking a Roman-inspired meal at home, reading a novel set in the city, or even starting to plan your return visit. Rome has a way of calling people back, and knowing that you'll see it again can soften the pang of departure. Until that time comes, the memories you've made, the lessons you've learned, and the connections you've formed will keep the city alive within you.

Leaving Rome is never easy, but it's a testament to the city's power to capture the hearts of those who visit. The memories you've created here are not fleeting; they are enduring echoes of a place that has left its mark on you. Farewells are not endings but beginnings of a new chapter, one where the Eternal City continues to inspire and accompany you, no matter where you are in the world.

CONCLUSION

Embracing the Eternal City: A Reflection

Rome is not a city you merely visit; it's a city you absorb, a city that becomes a part of you. Its streets, layered with centuries of history and humming with modern life, have a way of carving themselves into your memory. The Eternal City, with its unique blend of chaos and beauty, grandeur and intimacy, forces you to slow down, to look closer, and to feel deeper. It's a place that invites reflection not just on its history, but on your own experience within it. To embrace Rome is to embrace its contradictions, its imperfections, and its relentless charm. And long after you've left its cobblestone streets, the city's magic lingers, asking you to think back on what it gave, what it taught, and what it revealed.

The first thing that strikes most visitors about Rome is its sheer scale: the towering columns of the Pantheon, the colossal ruins of the Colosseum, and the sprawling magnificence of St. Peter's Basilica. These are not mere structures; they are monuments to human ambition and creativity, each one whispering the stories of those who came before us. Standing beneath the oculus of the Pantheon, for instance, you can't help but marvel at the ingenuity of ancient engineers who built something so enduring that it remains a centerpiece of modern Rome. Yet, it's not just the grandeur of these places that makes them memorable—it's their ability to make you feel small, to remind you of your place in the continuum of time. Walking through these spaces, you realize that Rome is both a city built by humans and one that transcends them, a paradox that challenges the way we think about legacy and permanence.

But Rome is not just about monumental landmarks. Its true essence often reveals itself in the smaller, quieter moments:

the faint scent of jasmine as you pass through a hidden courtyard, the way the light filters through the trees in Villa Borghese, or the sound of a street musician playing a haunting melody in a tucked-away piazza. These are the moments that catch you off guard, that fill you with an unexpected sense of connection to the city. It's in these fleeting experiences that you start to understand why Rome is called the Eternal City—not because it's frozen in time, but because it continues to live, breathe, and evolve in ways both big and small.

The people of Rome are an integral part of its character. Romans have a kind of effortless authenticity about them, a confidence born from living in a city that has seen it all. They are proud yet approachable, quick with a joke but earnest in their hospitality. Whether it's the barista who remembers your coffee order after one morning, the elderly woman who insists on giving you directions even if you didn't ask, or the shopkeeper who shares the story behind a leather bag you're considering, these interactions leave an indelible mark. Romans have mastered the art of living fully in the moment, and their energy is contagious. Spending time in their city teaches you to slow down, to savor, and to find joy in the everyday.

Rome also teaches resilience. This is a city that has been sacked, rebuilt, and reimagined countless times over the course of its history. Its ruins, far from being sad remnants of a lost past, are celebrations of survival and transformation. The Colosseum, battered but still standing, is a testament to the ingenuity of its builders and the endurance of its spirit. The Roman Forum, with its crumbling columns and fractured pediments, feels less like a ruin and more like a palimpsest—a place where the layers of history are visible all at once. Rome's ability to adapt while honoring its past is a lesson in resilience that resonates on both a personal and cultural level. It encourages you to see your own challenges as opportunities for growth and reinvention.

Food in Rome is more than a necessity; it's a way of life. From the simplicity of a perfectly cooked plate of carbonara to the complexity of a multi-course meal, Roman cuisine is a reflection of the city itself: honest, unpretentious, and deeply satisfying. Each meal becomes an opportunity to connect—not just with the flavors on your plate, but with the culture that created them. Sitting at a trattoria, watching the world go by as you sip a glass of local wine, you realize that meals in Rome are not rushed affairs. They are rituals, moments to pause, reflect, and enjoy. The act of sharing a meal with others, of breaking bread in a city that has done so for millennia, becomes a form of communion with the past and the present.

Rome also forces you to confront the concept of time in a way that few other cities can. Here, time feels both infinite and immediate. You might spend the morning exploring the ancient ruins of Palatine Hill, only to find yourself navigating the vibrant chaos of Campo de' Fiori in the afternoon. The juxtaposition of old and new is not jarring; rather, it feels natural, as if the city is reminding you that history and modernity are not opposing forces but complementary ones. This interplay of past and present encourages you to think about your own timeline, about the choices you make and the legacy you leave behind.

As you reflect on your time in Rome, you may find that the moments that stand out the most are not the ones you meticulously planned but the ones that happened by chance. Perhaps it was the unexpected kindness of a stranger or the serendipitous discovery of a quiet church where you sat for a moment of solitude. These unplanned experiences, small as they may seem, are the ones that often leave the deepest impressions. They remind you that travel is not just about ticking off sights on a list but about being open to the possibilities that each day brings.

Leaving Rome is never easy, but the city has a way of staying with you. Its lessons, its beauty, and its spirit become a part of your own story, shaping the way you see the world. The Eternal City doesn't just leave you with memories; it leaves you with a new perspective, a reminder of what it means to live fully, to connect deeply, and to appreciate the richness of life. And as you look back on your time there, you realize that Rome is not just a place you visited—it's a place that changed you.

Staying Connected with Rome: Future Adventures

The memories of Rome, with its labyrinthine streets, awe-inspiring monuments, and vibrant culture, have a way of staying with you long after you've left. But for many travelers, the thought of leaving such a unique and deeply impactful city can feel bittersweet. Rome has a magnetic pull, drawing you back even as you move on to new destinations or return to the routines of your daily life. Staying connected to the Eternal City is not just a matter of nostalgia—it's a way to deepen your appreciation of its influence and keep the door open for future adventures. Whether through cultural immersion, planning your next trip, or weaving the essence of Rome into your everyday life, there are countless ways to maintain your relationship with this remarkable city.

One of the simplest and most enriching ways to stay connected with Rome is by continuing to explore its culture from afar. Italian food, with its emphasis on fresh ingredients and bold yet simple flavors, provides an accessible gateway to revisiting the city. Experimenting with Roman recipes at home can transport you back to the trattorias and bustling markets you encountered during your visit. Dishes like carbonara, amatriciana, or saltimbocca alla Romana are not only delicious but also steeped in tradition, offering an opportunity to relive the sensory experiences of Rome. Sourcing authentic ingredients, such as Pecorino Romano cheese or guanciale, adds an extra layer of authenticity to your culinary creations. Cooking these meals becomes more than just a task—it becomes a ritual, a way to relive the moments you spent savoring Rome's gastronomic treasures.

Books and films set in Rome also provide a powerful means of reconnecting with the city. Diving into literature that captures the spirit of Rome allows you to see it through the eyes of others, offering fresh perspectives and insights. Whether it's historical fiction that brings ancient Rome to life, memoirs that reflect on the city's modern complexities, or travelogues that recount personal journeys, these works act as bridges to the Eternal City. Films, too, can evoke the magic of Rome. Watching iconic movies like *La Dolce Vita* or *Roman Holiday* can spark memories of your own experiences, while newer releases set in the city might inspire you to explore places you missed during your visit. These stories, whether written or visual, serve as reminders that Rome is not just a place—it's a living, breathing entity with a narrative that continues to unfold.

Staying connected to Rome also means keeping its art and history alive in your life. Visiting museums or exhibitions related to Roman culture, even in your home country, can be a deeply rewarding experience. Many major cities host traveling exhibitions of Roman artifacts, from ancient sculptures and mosaics to Renaissance paintings inspired by the city's artistic heritage. These exhibits often provide new context or details you may not have encountered during your time in Rome, enriching your understanding of its significance. If visiting in person isn't possible, many museums, including some in Rome, offer virtual tours and online archives that allow you to explore their collections from anywhere in the world. These resources ensure that your connection to the city remains dynamic and evolving.

Learning Italian, even at a basic level, is another meaningful way to stay tethered to Rome. Language is a window into culture, and picking up Italian phrases or delving deeper into the language can enhance your appreciation of the city. Whether you take formal classes, use language apps, or join local Italian-speaking groups, the process of learning Italian keeps Rome's rhythms and sounds fresh in your mind. You'll find that even small milestones, such as being able to order a meal in Italian or read a Roman street sign, bring a sense of accomplishment and a deeper connection to the city's essence. Plus, when you do return to Rome, your efforts will enrich your interactions with locals and open up new opportunities for meaningful exchanges.

Social media and technology offer another avenue for staying engaged with Rome. Following local photographers, historians, or cultural organizations on platforms like Instagram or Facebook allows you to see the city through the eyes of those who live there. These accounts often share stunning images of Roman landmarks, updates on cultural events, or little-known stories about the city's history. Engaging with these posts keeps you informed and inspired, while also fostering a sense of community with others who share your love for Rome. Similarly, listening to podcasts or watching documentaries about the city can deepen your understanding of its many layers, from its ancient origins to its modern identity.

Planning your next visit to Rome is perhaps the most exciting way to stay connected. Even if your return isn't immediate, the act of imagining future adventures can be incredibly fulfilling. Reflect on what you loved most about your first visit and consider what you'd like to explore further. Maybe you missed out on the Vatican Gardens or didn't have enough time to fully immerse yourself in the neighborhood of Trastevere. Perhaps you want to delve deeper into Roman history, exploring lesser-known archaeological sites like the Baths of Caracalla or the Appian Way. Creating a list of places to see, restaurants to try, or experiences to have ensures that your connection to Rome remains active and forward-looking.

Incorporating elements of Roman philosophy and lifestyle into your daily routine can also help you maintain a sense of connection. Rome teaches us the value of balance, of combining work with leisure, and of finding beauty in both the grand and the ordinary. Adopting these principles can be as simple as taking the time to enjoy a leisurely meal, setting aside moments for reflection, or appreciating the architecture and history of your own surroundings. These practices, inspired by your time in Rome, can transform the way you approach life, grounding you in the lessons the city has to offer.

Sharing your experiences of Rome with others is another powerful way to keep the city alive in your heart. Whether you're recounting stories to friends and family, writing a travel blog, or creating photo albums, these acts of storytelling allow you to relive your memories while inspiring others to discover Rome for themselves. Your perspective, shaped by your unique journey, adds to the collective narrative of the city. And as you share, you may find yourself reconnecting with details you'd forgotten, deepening your own appreciation of the experiences that made your time in Rome so special.

Rome is a city that thrives on connection—connection to its past, its people, and its visitors. By finding ways to stay engaged with the Eternal City, you ensure that it remains a part of your life, a source of inspiration and joy. Whether through culture, language, or planning your next adventure, the bond you've formed with Rome can continue to grow, reminding you that the city is always there, waiting to welcome you back.

BONUS 1: ESSENTIAL PHRASES FOR YOUR DAILY TRAVEL NEEDS IN ROME

BONUS 2: PRINTABLE TRAVEL JOURNAL

BONUS 3: 10 TIPS "THAT CAN SAVE THE DAY" ON YOUR TRIP IN ROME

Printed in Great Britain
by Amazon